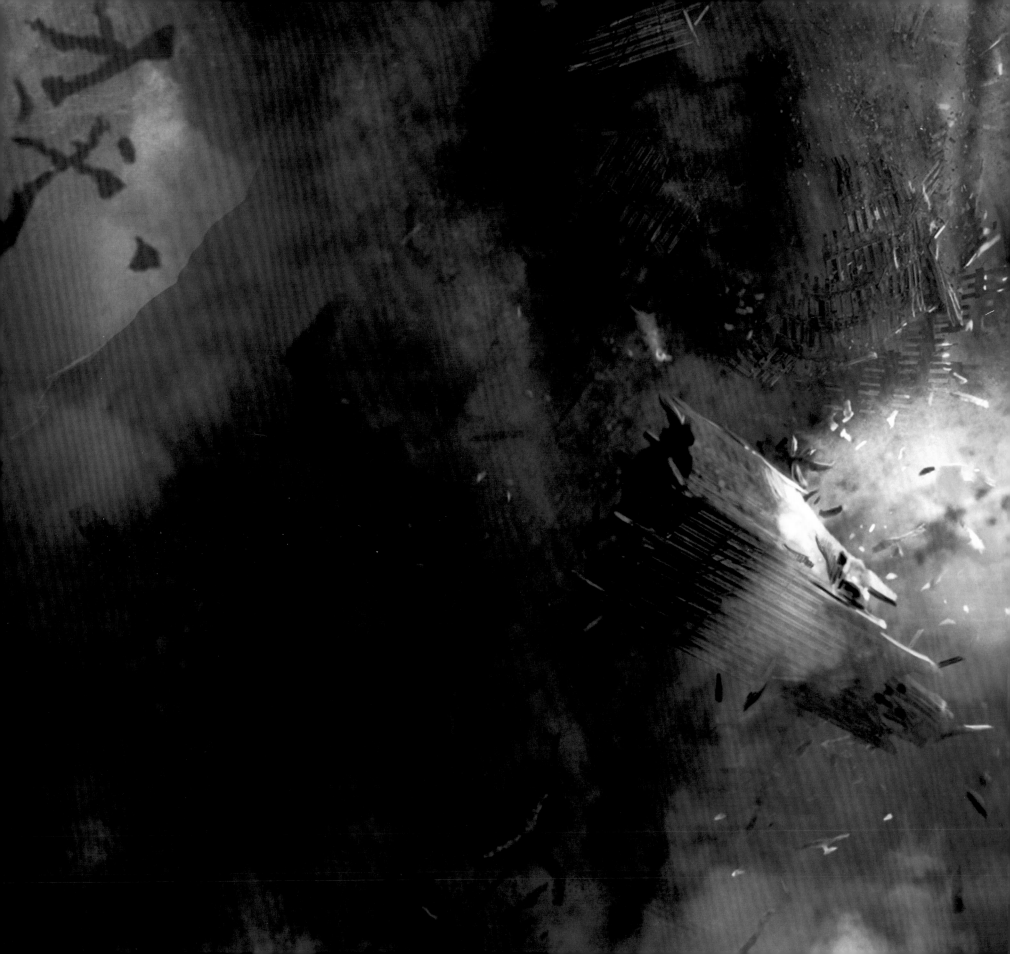

GODZILLA
THE ART OF DESTRUCTION

MARK COTTA VAZ

INSIGHT
EDITIONS

San Rafael, California

CONTENTS

GARETH EDWARDS

WRITING AN INTRODUCTION TO THIS BOOK is a bit of a dream come true. If you looked at my bookshelf at home, you wouldn't see many novels or screenplays, as every spare bit of real estate is largely taken up with "art of" books.

As soon as a new concept art book comes out, I head straight to the nearest comic shop and desperately turn the pages, trying to find any cool designs or ideas that didn't make the cut. I look at the development of a design or concept art for a shot and think, "Why didn't you pick that one? Why is that shot cut out? It's much better than the one that ended up in the movie! . . . What are these filmmakers thinking?"

I promised myself that if I ever got to make a film I wouldn't be so "stupid." If I was lucky enough to ever have an "art of" book, then I would make sure that every single beautiful shot or cool composition would end up on-screen. No one's talents would ever go to waste! . . . How wrong I was.

Going from my previous movie, an ultra low-budget indie film, to a prestigious blockbuster like *Godzilla* was a big risk for a studio. I owe a lot to Legendary (especially Thomas Tull) and Warner Bros. for sending me on this epic journey.

When Legendary called and asked me to send through some names of people I wanted to work with, my eyes lit up, and I just turned to my shelf and listed all my artistic heroes and kept my fingers crossed they would be available. I remember hearing that a lot of the responses were the same—many artists were obviously not available due to busy work commitments—but as soon as they heard it was *Godzilla*, the response was often "When do you want me to start?"

So as you will see, I ended up with a bit of an artistic dream team. From production designer Owen Paterson and his insanely talented team in Vancouver (led by Grant Van Der Slagt), through Weta Workshop (Andrew Baker, Christian Pearce, and Greg Broadmore), Steambot Studios (Sebastien Larroude), Legacy, my heroes Ryan Church and Erik Tiemens, Gavin Bocquet and his team (including Rob Bliss and Dominic Lavery), all the talented artists at MPC and Double Negative, to Steve Messing and my now good friend Matt Allsopp, whose DNA is all over this movie, just to name a few, . . . I felt I had died and gone to "art of" heaven. I figured, even if this film completely bombed, at least we'd have a beautiful behind-the-scenes book!

People talk about directors having a "vision," which I always think sounds very pretentious. But things often get caught in your peripheral vision, and it's the job of the artists in this book to bring them into focus. Art is not a science; there is no right or wrong, but there is definitely a "better" or "worse." So for me, design is a lot like an evolution. You start with a crude, simple organism, then try lots of experiments and mutations of an image, trying to find that happy accident that evolves it onto the next level. It's those accidents, the real breakthroughs, that you

PART ONE

DREAMING

ATOMIC MONSTER 核怪獣

THE FIRST ATOMIC BOMB WAS DETONATED during the early dawn of a summer day in 1945, out in the rugged New Mexico desert. Ten thousand yards from ground zero a blinding, white-hot flash lasted almost two minutes. An earth-shattering boom that an Army general at base camp remembered as a "deep growling roar" followed. As an unearthly cloud rose, seemingly poised to drift out and engulf them, the general noted the relief on the face of the physicist who had been lying facedown outside the control bunker—his look said *it worked*. Another observer subsequently recalled seeing that brilliant physicist, J. Robert Oppenheimer—who led the Manhattan Project that built the bomb—and never forgot his walk. It was the walk of a man in control of his destiny, like the lawman out of *High Noon*—"this kind of strut. He had done it." The atomic bomb was meant for Hitler, but with Nazi Germany's defeat, America unleashed its newfound atomic power on the remaining Axis foe, Japan, decimating the cities of Hiroshima and Nagasaki. The atomic destruction marked the horrifying end of a campaign of total war.[1]

The Atomic Age was soon reflected in the dream world of popular culture. In the movies, atomic monsters became a favored metaphor. The first to emerge was a prehistoric creature that had slumbered beneath Arctic ice until awakened by a nuclear bomb test. As if to punish humanity for its clumsy tinkering with cosmic forces, the creature wreaked havoc on the city that had risen on its primordial spawning grounds. This creature-that-time-forgot made the Warner Bros. release *The Beast from 20,000 Fathoms* one of the smash hits of 1953.

In November 1954 Toho of Japan released another of what have been called "the big-lizard movies."[2] It was a memorable year for Toho, with its release of *Seven Samurai*, a period epic that remains a masterpiece of world cinema. Toho probably had no such aspirations for *Gojira* [translated as *Godzilla*]. Their towering creature from the Jurassic period, arisen from the deep ocean and crackling with nuke test radiation, was brought to life as a man in a rubber suit stomping a scale miniature Tokyo. But, in reality, the film was a dark and disturbing reflection on what science had wrought. The ensuing franchise, which later lost that dark edge, became one of the most successful in movie history, with close to thirty Toho films and a 1998 American version from Sony TriStar.

For some time, it seemed as if Godzilla had disappeared, slumbering out of sight if not mind. He would once again be awakened in 2014, having gestated under the care of Legendary Pictures, when Warner Bros. joined Legendary in a co-production that promised "an epic rebirth to Toho's iconic Godzilla."

Screenwriter Max Borenstein had watched *Gojira* and its sequels as a kid. When Legendary tapped him as a key *Godzilla* screenwriter, he revisited *Gojira*. The film opens with a flash of atomic fire destroying a fishing boat at sea—a reference to *Daigo Fukuryu Maru*, the Japanese tuna fishing boat exposed to radiation from a nuclear test on Bikini Atoll in March 1954. Godzilla's atomic ray later turns Tokyo into a sea of fire, a horrifying reminder to Japanese audiences of what they had endured a few years before. In one scene, billowing flames fill Tokyo's nocturnal sky and a weeping mother, holding her children tightly, exclaims, "We'll be joining your father. . . ."

LEFT The nuclear detonatio
opens *Godzilla* recalls the
Atoll atomic test of 1954
in turn, inspired Toho's s
Gojira. **OPPOSITE** Concept
Matt Allsopp created this ima
a Warner Bros. presentatio
original black-and-white v
was colored and then blown
immense size for the show.

"And you *know* Daddy died in World War II!," Borenstein says. "It's a pretty masterful movie, but also a very intense sociological document of its time. Godzilla is a force of nature and clearly a metaphor for the nuclear aftermath of World War II and bomb tests in the South Pacific. Coming at a time when it feels that every year we get a horrible disaster, from hurricanes to tsunamis and nuclear meltdowns, the notion that when you tamper with nature you get untold consequences [feels] incredibly resonant."

The underlying themes, and the focus on the human drama, helped attract an all-star cast, including Bryan Cranston (star of the AMC television series *Breaking Bad*) and Aaron Taylor-Johnson (*Savages*, the *Kick-Ass* movies), who play father and son, Joe and Ford Brody, respectively, and whose troubled relationship becomes entwined with the emergence of the new atomic monsters. In a nod to *Gojira*, Ken Watanabe (*Letters from Iwo Jima, Inception*) was cast as Dr. Ishiro Serizawa, named in honor of the tortured scientist from the original film. In true *Godzilla* tradition, military forces are called upon to slay the monster, with David Strathairn as the admiral who leads the troops.

"Sure, it's a monster movie that's going to have mind-boggling computer-generated effects," reflects Strathairn, whose recent roles include Secretary of State William Seward in *Lincoln*. "But I think it's much more potent than that, and that's why it's had such lasting power. *Godzilla* struck a very personal note for the United States and Japan. And the fact that Japan made this film nine years after the bomb was, to me, extraordinary, an incredibly courageous and audacious thing to do. They brought this symbolic creature into our consciousness. It's a very poetic construct, a symbol for so many things we are still working on as a species."

"AN EPIC REBIRTH TO TOHO'S ICONIC GODZILLA"

"I wouldn't be here if it was just, '*Look out, this monster is crushing everything!*'" adds Cranston, whose *Breaking Bad* won the Primetime Emmy® Award for Outstanding Drama Series during *Godzilla*'s post-production. "Instead of trying to humanize the beast, what this film does—and, I think, rightfully so—is humanize the people. You root for them and sympathize with their plight. And the cross-generational component [of his and Aaron's characters] really worked for me."

Director of photography Seamus McGarvey, who recently filmed the global blockbuster *The Avengers*, was fascinated by the underlying themes: "There was something very exciting about it sort of criticizing man's hubris. I think it's a very politically relevant film in terms of colonization and war, in terms of our blindness in trampling over the place where we live. That was the thing that immediately attracted me to do this film. It's not going to wear its politics on its sleeve, but it's a film with contemporary relevance."

Legendary CEO and studio founder Thomas Tull helped develop the property with Legendary president and producer Jon Jashni, and Legendary executive and *Godzilla* executive producer Alex Garcia.

Tull, whose recent productions include *Pacific Rim*, *42*, and *The Dark Knight Rises*, explains that Toho "entrusted" them with the character. This was more than a movie deal. "I've been a huge Godzilla fan since I was a kid," he says. "As an eight-year-old, I certainly didn't understand the significance of it coming out of Japan after World War II. It was simply for me the idea that this creature would appear, be godlike, personify nature, and you just had to try to survive it. Of course, when it got to fight other creatures later on, that was pretty awesome, too. It was such an incredible concept. We wanted to make sure we got the story right and gave this first-class treatment."

For the production team, the attraction was resurrecting one of the few characters whose renown has endured for more than half a century. "We like to say we are 'source-agnostic,'" says Jashni. "We don't care where the inspiration comes from—whether it's an original idea, from another medium entirely, or a remake of a classic film. We strive to be authentic, to begin with the building blocks of story, irrespective of where the ideas come from. In the case of Godzilla, in 1954 the same resources obviously didn't exist to create the kind of Godzilla you can create today. We wanted to make the definitive *Godzilla* in terms of resources, approach, and love for the canon without being completely slavish to what came before. We wanted to present *Godzilla* as it needs and deserves to be for today's audiences."

"HE IS KING OF THE MONSTERS AND INDESTRUCTIBLE, BUT THERE'S A REAL DUALITY TO HIS CHARACTER."

Garcia notes a parallel with Legendary and Warner Bros.' updating of the Batman franchise with *The Dark Knight Trilogy*. "How do you take a character who has a lot of baggage and has had different incarnations over the years and reintroduce what made him great?" Garcia muses. "We wanted to get to the pure center of Godzilla."

"Godzilla has attained its iconic status and universal appeal for a number of reasons," concludes veteran producer Mary Parent, one of the key members of the *Godzilla* production team. "On a primal level, all his roaring and stomping is tremendously fun. He is King of the Monsters and indestructible, but there's a real duality to his character—he's as much a hero as he is a villain and does everything with such a devil-may-care attitude."

ABOVE Godzilla on ice, concept art. A Godzilla carcass was to have been discovered entombed in Siberia, but that changed

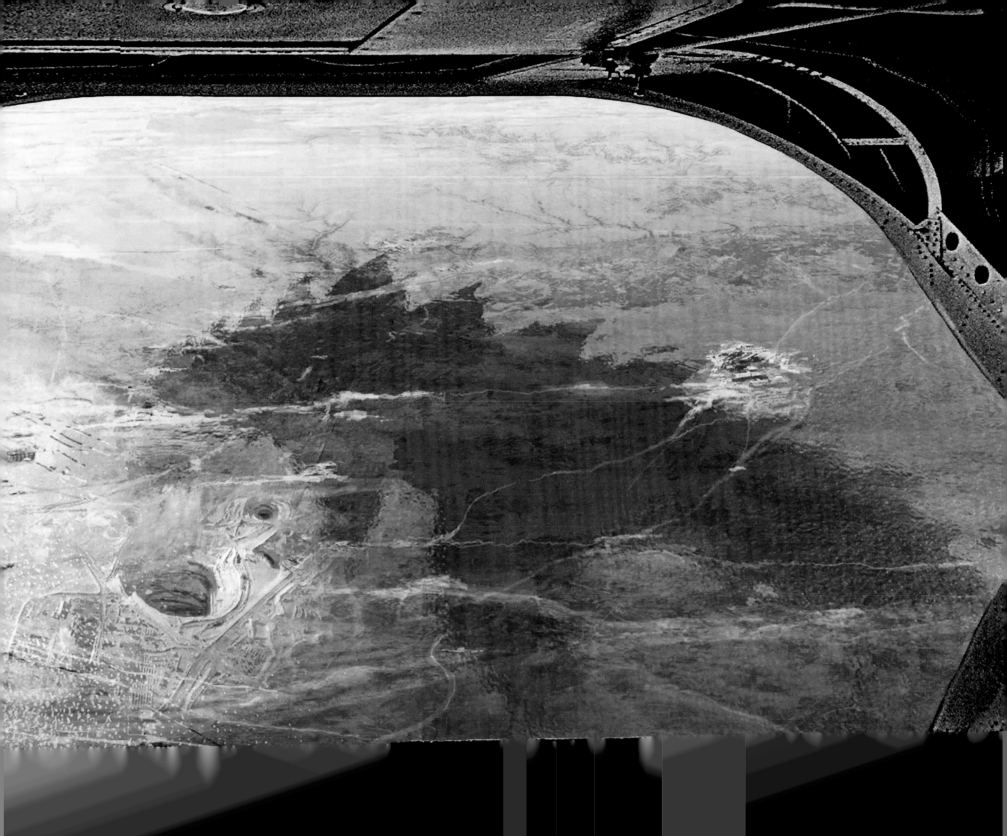

Leading the behind-the-camera talent was director Gareth Edwards, a young filmmaker from England with only one picture on his résumé, a low-budget, independent 2010 Vertigo Films release called *Monsters*. *Monsters*, set six years after an alien invasion, follows a young male photojournalist and the daughter of a media mogul as they journey north through Central America to the border of Mexico and the United States, where military forces have contained the creatures to the "Infected Zone." The aliens are only briefly glimpsed—*Monsters* is, essentially, "a road movie that masquerades as a genre movie," Borenstein observes. The entire production team consisted of Edwards and a handful of people traveling through Central America, shooting on the fly. Edwards not only wrote and directed, he also filmed it all with a digital camera and created the visual effects.

The *Godzilla* producers also assembled a high-powered team that included two-time Oscar®-nominated cinematographer Seamus McGarvey (*Anna Karenina*, *The Avengers*, *Atonement*), production designer Owen Paterson (*V for Vendetta*, the *Matrix* trilogy), two-time Oscar®-nominated costume designer Sharen Davis (*Django Unchained*, *Dreamgirls*, *Ray*), and two-time Oscar®-nominated sound designer Erik Aadahl (*Argo*, *The Tree of Life*, the *Transformers* trilogy) and Oscar®-winning supervising sound editor Ethan Van der Ryn (*The Lord of the Rings* trilogy, *World War Z*). Also recruited was three-time Oscar®-winning visual effects supervisor Jim Rygiel (*The Lord of the Rings* trilogy, *The Amazing Spider-Man*), whose effects effort included the work of The Moving Picture Company (MPC), Double Negative (DNeg), and other storied visual effects studios.

When camera operator Mitch Dubin, who had worked with McGarvey on *The Avengers*, was asked to join *Godzilla*, he was curious about the virtually unknown director. He watched *Monsters* and was impressed, particularly at the end credits: "Gareth did *everything*! There are no credits for camera assistant, camera operators, gaffers, grips, props. Gareth did his own visual effects. I'm confident in saying that filmmaking is a collaborative process, but maybe Gareth is the exception. He did what I thought was impossible—he was a one-man band. But I was concerned about the transition of him going from *Monsters* to a big-budget movie with a huge crew."

How could a filmmaker from England whose only feature had been an art-house take on the alien invasion genre, handle a big-budget Hollywood blockbuster that aimed to resurrect one of the most iconic movie monsters in film history?

Dubin was one of many converts: "I think certain people have filmmaking as part of their DNA. It's like they're born filmmakers. And that's what Gareth is."

LEFT Godzilla being dug out from the ice, Siberia scene concept art. "The original idea was to find Godzilla and another creature interlocked and frozen in battle," director Gareth Edwards recalls, "as if they'd been frozen in time for millions of years. The only problem with that is that from a silhouette point of view, it would neither look like a Godzilla or a MUTO; it would be this strange mess seen through the ice, so it wouldn't work."

JOURNEY STORY

GARETH EDWARDS AND HIS TWO ACTORS had climbed the ancient steps of a Mayan temple to film a moody twilight-to-nightfall sequence for *Monsters*. As Edwards was filming, actor Scoot McNairy got concerned that his director was drifting too close to the edge. "I was aware of where the edge was, but I was more worried about making the shots," Edwards admits. "But we went through a lot of situations that could have ended a lot worse for us. We were going through drug cartel areas, and there were shootings. We turned up on one street where eleven coffins were in the middle of the street, by the police station, because someone had just shot everyone in this café. There's a strange contrast in Central America, which we tried to put in the film, where just around the corner there was potential destruction, but where you are there's beautiful people that are friendly and seem very happy. It doesn't quite add up. It should be a bleak thing, but it's not that simple. I liked that contrast. You've got something horrific, and you try to find something innocent in it."

As a child growing up in the midlands of England, Edwards wore out the family's Betamax videocassette copy of *Star Wars*. He recalls his nearly daily immersions in the 1977 saga of Luke Skywalker, Han Solo, Princess Leia, and the Rebel Alliance's battle against the Empire as a kind of training film for his own future service. "I grew up wanting to join the Rebel Alliance and blow up the Death Star," he recalls. "Gradually, it became clear *Star Wars* was a thing called a 'movie.' I genuinely wanted to be a filmmaker from when I knew there were such things as films."

Edwards concludes that one of the reasons *Star Wars* so entranced him and other generations was that it sounded the mythic, and universal, themes of the hero's journey: "*Star Wars* was the ultimate hero's journey, where something is wrong at home and you leave and venture out into a special world. As humans we're sort of born with the hardware, but we haven't got the software yet. Our parents, our elders, the previous generation go off to risk their lives and do things, so that when it's your turn to face those challenges you hopefully choose the right thing to be successful. I think that's why, on the whole, we're attracted to stories with happy endings. When people say a story is pointless, they mean it's not useful, that you can't learn anything from it."

"YOU'VE GOT SOMETHING HORRIFIC, AND YOU TRY TO FIND SOMETHING INNOCENT IN IT."

LEFT Gareth Edwards checks out a key Godzilla maquette. For the young director, the *Godzilla* assignment was a dream come true. OPPOSITE The director prepares for a scene with Ken Watanabe, whose character, Dr. Serizawa, is the conscience of the story. "He's basically Godzilla's savior," says fellow cast member David Strathairn.

Edwards' own journey story would take him to Hollywood, a trip that is itself a mythic construct—the starry-eyed newcomer, freshly arrived in Tinseltown, dreaming of stardom. But for Edwards, the scenario was more like a stranger in a strange land. "It's weird now that I'm in L.A.," Edwards says. "In England we associate America with a lot of the films we grew up with, so it's very strange to come live here. I spend the whole time thinking I'm in one big movie set. It's very strange."

Edwards arrived with some experience climbing the ropes of the British television and film industry, including previous work in visual effects. It was a humble beginning—on one British TV show, he'd get up before dawn to make tea for everybody and then run errands all day. He admittedly made *Monsters* to further his career, but he was philosophical: If his movie went nowhere, at least he had tried; if he was lucky, maybe someone would ask him to make another.

In 2010, when *Monsters* was screened at the Alamo Drafthouse Cinema in Austin, Texas, an agent in attendance, Mike Simpson from William Morris Endeavor, was impressed enough to offer to represent Gareth. "So I came to L.A., and they organized, like, a million interviews for me," Edwards recalls. "I had to drive around like a madman to all these different meetings. I was perpetually late and constantly apologizing."

Edwards visited Legendary Pictures and met studio founder and producer Thomas Tull, who offered him a home at Legendary. "Thomas was saying everything you wanted to hear, which really threw me," says Edwards.

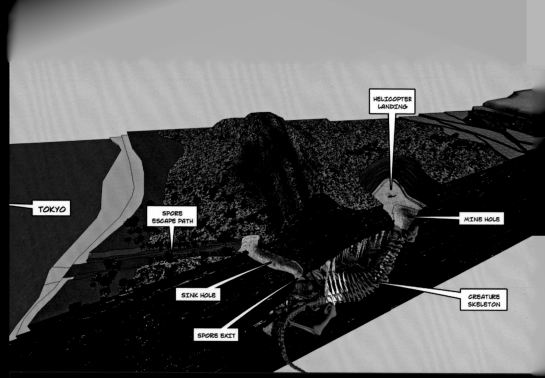

ABOVE The Siberia locale was changed to a mine in the Philippines. This schematic plots out the site of an ancient creature, harbinger of the radioactive monsters about to be reawakened. BELOW Further Siberia scene concept art, unused in the final film. OPPOSITE Aerial view concept art of the Philippine mine created by the art team in Vancouver. "Instead of having this sequence on ice, the Philippine mine was more [in keeping with] our theme about the destruction of nature," Edwards notes. "In the long run, it was actually for the better, because it reflected the man-versus-nature theme that's predominant throughout the film."

Six months later, Tull called Edwards and asked if he would be willing to take on "a massive movie franchise." Edwards replied that it depended on the project. A few days later, he got an urgent email from his agency asking that he call as soon as possible. Calling from his home in London, Edwards was told by his agent, Rich Cook, to make sure he was sitting down. Legendary wanted to know if Edwards would be interested in directing *Godzilla*. "I was sort of quiet," he recalls. "What was weird was I was about to watch my copy of the 1954 black-and-white Japanese film. It was sitting on my table. And they asked, 'Do you like it?' I said, 'Yeah. I'm looking at it right now.'"

THE FIRST TIME I MET GARETH, THERE WAS A QUIET CONFIDENCE ABOUT HIM THAT I THINK YOU HAVE TO HAVE TO BE A SUCCESSFUL DIRECTOR. "

The journey to that moment began in 2005, when independent producer Brian Rogers, a specialist in 3-D productions (*Harry Potter and the Deathly Hallows: Part 2*) met Kenji Okuhira and his partner, director Yoshimitsu Banno, at a conference on large-format film. Okuhira and Banno had obtained a licensing agreement from Toho to produce a sixty-minute 3-D Godzilla film for IMAX theaters. Rogers immediately signed on.

In June 2005, Banno came to Los Angeles and the 3-D Godzilla project began moving forward. It quickly became obvious that the new and emerging technology was perfect for

the outsized atomic creature. "I saw that digital projection was going to revolutionize the way theater audiences were going to see a 3-D picture," Rogers says. "IMAX and digital projection was moving into the mainstream. So, in the fall of 2006, we set up a meeting with Toho to convert the original agreement to a feature-film American agreement. . . The negotiations were concluded shortly before Legendary Pictures' formal acquisition of *Godzilla* in March of 2010."

Rogers adds that although there was widespread interest throughout Hollywood in reviving *Godzilla*, only Legendary seemed to have the passion to undertake the creative journey. "Thomas Tull at Legendary had grown up with the franchise and was personally interested in breathing new life into it," Rogers says. "Thomas completely got it."

Although Legendary had already commissioned a *Godzilla* screenplay, when Gareth Edwards showed up on the studio's radar, the process truly began moving forward. "When I was told how much *Monsters* cost—and how much Gareth had done on his laptop—I was blown away," says Tull. "The first time I met Gareth, there was a quiet confidence about him that I think you have to have to be a successful director. We just hit it off and we thought, 'Let's get our field general, our director, and build this out from there.' That's when we reached out to Gareth."

Legendary's Jon Jashni observes that the meager budget and other constraints of *Monsters*, and the way Edwards overcame those limitations, made him an ideal candidate for directing *Godzilla*, despite its mega-budget and challenges. "Just because you can throw a ton of digital resources at the screen doesn't mean you should, as it doesn't really aid audience connectivity or immersion in the world you're trying to create," Jashni says. "On *Monsters* Gareth had to suggest a lot more than he could afford to show. He came from a character-based perspective, grounded in the real world, and then layered otherworldly elements into that world. *Monsters* was microcosmic of what we hoped to create with our new Godzilla movie, real and true."

"Certainly, dealing with a movie of this logistical complexity and marshaling all the assets—a big budget, large cast, tons of visual effects—can be overwhelming," adds Legendary's Alex Garcia. "It was a huge leap, but we never blinked with Gareth."

In the autumn of 2011, the director was hooked up with Max Borenstein. "They picked Gareth, who made a movie several orders of magnitude less than this, because they believed in him and he made something off the beaten path," says Borenstein. "It felt, after my initial conversation with Gareth and the studio, that it was a cautionary tale about man tampering with nature."

The director and screenwriter engaged in marathon Skype story sessions connecting Edwards in London and Borenstein in Los Angeles. However, they embarked on the project in the aftermath of the 9.0 magnitude earthquake and tsunami that led to the nuclear disaster at Japan's Fukushima Daiichi nuclear power plant. Sensitive to that unfolding disaster, there was discussion about not beginning the film in Japan. The U.S. and Korea were contemplated, Edwards says, but it was finally decided *Godzilla* had to begin in the land of the monster's birth. Japan's nuclear crisis only made more relevant the themes of humankind's destructive hubris and the fragile nature of the modern world.

"It's not so much a monster movie as a disaster movie," Borenstein notes. "We were also resonant with 9/11. Our idea was, how do you make this movie tap into some of these visceral feelings that we've all had about being powerless, to try to use a monster movie to get at deeper emotions? All that stuff was swimming around."

"IT'S NOT SO MUCH A MONSTER MOVIE AS A DISASTER MOVIE.

Legendary also wanted another giant monster in the mix. "In all honesty, it's such a crazy scenario," Edwards says. "It's hard enough trying to get Godzilla realistically into the world, let alone two creatures! An audience might accept that Godzilla exists, but other creatures? Could that become silly?"

Edwards realized they had creative freedom in a character endowed with the mythic power of Godzilla: "It's a giant monster, but you can kind of paint any picture you want. There are as many potential stories as there are westerns or war movies, or anything that involves some threat to a society. It's an infinite canvas, really."

BRAINSTORMING

THE GODZILLA STORY CONFERENCE CALLS often lasted ten hours or more, beginning in late morning for Max Borenstein in Los Angeles, which was early evening in London for Gareth Edwards. They had their mandates and a few ground rules. First, they wanted the fantastical events to unfold in the real world. The story would have the requisite presence of scientists and soldiers, but there would be no superior character representing humankind's lone hope to stop the monster. Borenstein's inspiration for their central character was the 1977 classic, *Close Encounters of the Third Kind*, wherein Richard Dreyfuss plays an ordinary man drawn into a cosmic drama. "Instead of having a character who is the only person who can possibly stop the threat, the more interesting story that felt plausible was for a character that ends up being *that guy*," Borenstein explains. "For the character, it's closure. You have a sense of inevitability, but it's grounded. He's an everyman following his own course."

"This is the thing—you don't really keep score," Edwards says. "But I'm pretty sure Max came up with the idea of the nuclear reactor meltdown."

The first draft tied the ostensible meltdown into a cover-up and a subsequent revelation of a monster that feeds off radiation; the twist was, it would not be Godzilla, but another creature. The director and writer then imagined a journey back, years later, to the nuclear facility, now a restricted area and a place of secrets.

This monster would be called a MUTO, an acronym for "Massive Unidentified Terrestrial Organism." The original script, prior to Edwards' involvement, had posited a similar creature as Godzilla's ancient antagonist but had not established *why* they were enemies. "We thought, 'What if the other creatures had a kind of parasitic relationship to Godzilla?'" Edwards recalls. "When these Godzillas were on Earth, there was another creature that would kill them and lay [its] eggs inside [their dead bodies]. Therefore, if these creatures ever came back, part of their life cycle would be the ability to attract Godzillas to the surface to kill [them] for reproduction. So we decided that would be the way to go."

In their backstory, Godzilla and the MUTO go back 250 million years. Earth's atmosphere was still developing, the planet was highly radioactive, and creatures depended on radiation for their life cycle in the same way plants absorb and photosynthesize sunlight. In that savage, primordial world, Godzilla was the alpha predator. A single MUTO could not defeat a Godzilla, but they learned to hunt in packs. After killing a Godzilla, the MUTOs would lay their spores in their victim's radioactive carcass. "It will almost certainly not wind up in the movie, or it might be hinted at, but it felt very important for us to have a plausible reason to explain that their motivations were akin to animals," Borenstein explains. "We release the MUTOs, and that calls up Godzilla."

By March 2012, Edwards and Borenstein had a first draft. Legendary now urged Edwards to begin fleshing out key scenes, beginning with the 3-D conceptual "previsualization" animation process, so they would have something to show their production partner Warner Bros. that would get them on board with

the production. The director decided that for the big presentation he wanted to show a face-off between Godzilla and the MUTO in Hawaii. It first had to be storyboarded—enter Matt Allsopp, a concept artist living in London who hailed from Edwards' hometown (a fact the two discovered later in the production). Not only would Allsopp storyboard the Hawaii sequence, but he would also help design Godzilla and continue to board material in conjunction with development of the screenplay and previz sequences. "It was not a common process, the way it worked out," Borenstein notes. "It was a feedback cycle from storyboard to screenplay that ended up affecting a great deal of stuff."

> "THE MUTOS WOULD LAY THEIR SPORES IN THEIR VICTIM'S RADIOACTIVE CARCASS."

ABOVE Concept artist Matt Allsopp ponders the next creative move with Gareth Edwards. "He would contribute ideas and draw boards, and we'd just bounce it around," says Edwards. "It was probably one of the most enjoyable parts of the film." OPPOSITE Early concept art for the spore nest of a "Massive Unidentified Terrestrial Organism" (MUTO). "There's a simplicity to this image that I think makes it really strong and easy to understand," says Edwards. FOLLOWING PAGES Concept art for the top secret facility where the cocoon of a MUTO will hatch. "My justification for [the shape] was the way that plants grow toward the sun—they follow the line of the sun, so they grow straight up. But this creature uses electromagnetic waves, which, just like when you put iron filings on a magnet, curve around."

EVOLUTION 進化

ALL MATT ALLSOPP EVER WANTED TO DO—his "passion," as he puts it—was to make art, whether painting a traditional landscape or drawing spaceships and sci-fi fantasy. "My exercise books at school were just full of the doodles I'd be making while the teacher was talking," he says. "I'd get called up on that, but I could not stop drawing."

Some eleven years ago, when he was around seventeen and a year into college, he discovered books about movie concept art and realized he could meld his passion for art with his love of movies. Around the same time, he discovered the computer and Photoshop. "I bought a tablet and went 100 percent with the computer—that was massively, massively important," he recalls. "The tools now are amazing. Everything is at your fingertips."

His way into the business was the London-based Motion Picture Company. He did "little bits" for *Man of Steel*, but *Godzilla* would be his first really intense production. "It was a complete coincidence," Allsopp recalls. "One day, Gareth came to MPC's office and needed some storyboards very quickly. 'Well, Matt is free!' So they introduced me to Gareth and we clicked. It was brilliant. It went on from there."

"AS THE LIGHTS COME ON, THEY LIGHT UP THE MUTO STANDING OVER THE TRACK, AND THAT WAS GOING TO BE A BADASS MOMENT."

The rush job was for the Hawaii sequence and the previz required to make it part of the upcoming summer presentation to Warner Bros. "I don't think Matt had done storyboards before this film," Gareth Edwards says. "He's really a concept artist like his heroes, people like Syd Mead and Ryan Church. I think he didn't like the idea of doing storyboards; he felt they were a step down. But every one of his storyboards looked like a piece of concept art. They were black and white, but really polished. He's got this gift. If you took Matt out of the picture, stylistically this would be a different film."

That first set piece developed as a night scene on an airport monorail in Honolulu. The power goes out, stopping the monorail. The power comes back on, but just ahead on the tracks awaits a MUTO, a creature with the power to short out electricity. "As the lights come on, they light up the MUTO standing over the track, and that was going to be a badass moment," Borenstein recalls. "We came up with that idea in a Skype call, and the next day Gareth talked to Matt and they worked up visual gags for this sequence."

Parallel to the storyboarding and previz development of the Hawaii piece was an idea Edwards developed for a *Godzilla* teaser trailer. Edwards recalls the inspiration came during a meeting with Legendary's CEO Thomas Tull and president Jon Jashni. They were showing the director a clip of a CG Godzilla that had

THIS STILL LOOKS GREAT
LOVE THE 'HAPPY ACCIDENTS' OF THE RIBBING ETC

ONE REASON I THINK IT WORKS SO WELL
ARE MANY OF THE LINES FLOW AND MEET
OTHER LINES FROM OTHER BODY PARTS

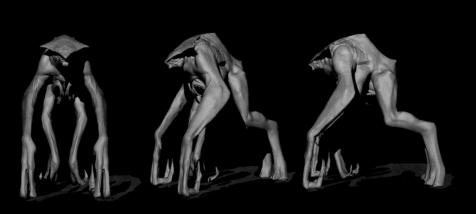

ABOVE AND LEFT From pencil lines to 3-D designs, Matt Allsopp, seen here in the Vancouver office, had a hand in the design of winged male and gigantic female MUTOs. FAR LEFT A joke illustration created for Edwards' assistant, Shannon Triplett, who had to organize the exhaustive back-and-forth between the director and Allsopp as they designed the MUTO. OPPOSITE TOP AND BOTTOM Sketches from the frenetic design process. "You wonder why some images look better than others," says Edwards, "and I think sometimes it's because the lines flow—there's a lot of lines in this design that, if you carried them on, they'd connect to other parts of the body, which make it feel more appealing."

THE MONORAIL BEGINS TO POWER BACK UP.

BULLETS FROM THE APACHE COME SMASHING THROUGH THE MONORAIL WINDOWS.

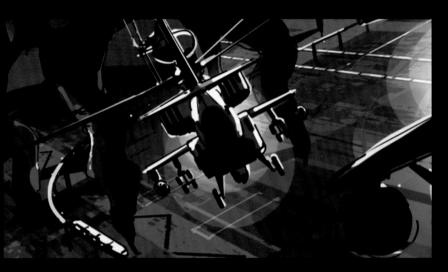

APACHE HELICOPTERS CAN NOW TARGET THE CREATURE.

THE TRAIN DOORS AUTOMATICALLY OPEN AS THE PASSENGERS HOLD ON FOR DEAR LIFE.

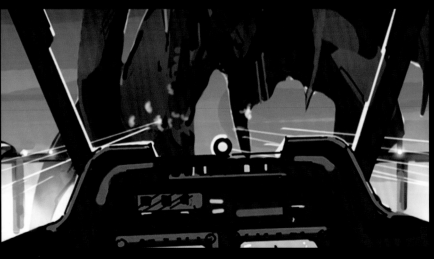

THEY FIRE EVERYTHING THEY HAVE TRYING TO KILL IT.

IT REACTS AND SMASHES THROUGH THE MONORAIL TRACK.

appeared in a Japanese movie, and Edwards casually remarked, "We can do better." "You're on," Tull said, in effect.

"I thought, 'Oh no, I've got to think up something now,'" says Edwards. "I think what they liked about that clip was Godzilla was in 3-D, in the style of the original fifties version. You could see the potential. Thomas said, 'Just propose something, and we'll find the money to do it.' But I was having a bit of writer's block."

Edwards then left on a scheduled business trip to Japan that included a visit to Toho. During his stop at the studio, he was given a gift of a photography book. It had nothing to do with Godzilla or Toho, but with writer's block and a looming deadline, he decided to use it as inspiration. Somewhere in this book, Edwards decided, is *the idea*. "This one image stood out," he says. "It was a photograph of a landslide falling down a waterfall, and the entire frame was filled with rock, debris, and dust. I pictured Godzilla slowly coming out of that debris. It was very September 11 in the way it might work."

Edwards also recalled visual effects work he had done for a BBC documentary on Hiroshima, a program that included a 1965 NBC documentary recording of Robert Oppenheimer's somber recollection of that first atomic blast in New Mexico: "We knew the world would not be the same. A few people laughed, a few people cried. Most people were silent. I remembered the line from the Hindu scripture, the Bhagavad-Gita; Vishnu is trying to persuade the prince that he should do his duty, and to impress him, takes on his multi-armed form and says, 'Now I become death, the destroyer of worlds.'"[3]

"I felt Oppenheimer's quote would be a good framework to hang these shots on," Edwards recalls. "I did a quick edit on my laptop, stealing shots from

Baraka, this epic art film, and typed some text over it. I sent it to Legendary and felt they would totally reject it because it wasn't popcorn enough. The feedback was, 'It's excellent. Do it.'"

Tull provided the promised funding and the director went to MPC to create a fully computer-generated teaser that would be a moody and tantalizing glimpse of the spirit of the movie. Guillaume Rocheron, MPC's future visual effects supervisor on *Godzilla*, was then busy supervising his company's work on *Man of Steel*, but recalls Edwards designed some six shots for a documentary-style look at a disaster's aftermath. The eerie scene included a strange, dead monster. But there was no doubt about the last monster standing; a dramatic reveal of a roaring Godzilla emerging from the smoke and ruins.

> ## "I FELT OPPENHEIMER'S QUOTE WOULD BE A GOOD FRAMEWORK TO HANG THESE SHOTS ON."

"MPC worked on it for months in their spare time," Edwards recalls. "I'd pop in every week, and we'd go through iterations. Everyone was putting so much time into the thing [that] the question became 'Is anyone going to see this?' It got better and better and, eventually, Legendary said, 'Let's take it to Comic-Con [in San Diego] as a big surprise.'"

Rocheron notes that, early on, it was agreed that MPC would not only provide visual effects, but be responsible for creating Godzilla and generating all

the Godzilla shots, as well as the MUTO. Ultimately, many hands would have a go at designing Godzilla and the other creature. Weta Digital was involved at the earliest stage, working up a CG Godzilla model, while Legacy crafted a physical maquette. Edwards worked closely with Weta designer Andrew Baker on a 3-D Godzilla sculpt, and felt they had gotten the design about 80 percent there, but he wanted to take it all the way.

Matt Allsopp recalls that one Sunday afternoon at home he took a crack at Godzilla's head design. At the time he hadn't made Edwards' acquaintance, but the next day he slipped his take into material MPC had prepared for Edwards' review. "Mine was the one he liked," says Allsopp. "It was about finding the right mix: If his head was too short he looked too doglike, if he was too long it looked a bit goofy. The thing I went for was quite aggressive looking. It looked a bit like an eagle in profile. It just really worked. And then I continued to work on Godzilla, and MUTO designs as well."

Allsopp had also been turning out storyboards for the Hawaii sequence, so it was time to push the imagery further in the 3-D previz process. But Edwards wasn't wild about this next stage of the production's evolution.

"Going into this, I really didn't want to do previz," the director admits. "I rolled my eyes when they brought it up. I felt like it was going to create this unspontaneous way of telling a story, because you have to animate months before you even stand on location with the actors."

> ## "IT WAS ABOUT FINDING THE RIGHT MIX: IF HIS HEAD WAS TOO SHORT HE LOOKED TOO DOGLIKE IF IT WAS TOO LONG IT LOOKED A BIT GOOFY."

Legendary had worked with The Third Floor, a previz company, and they were called in to work with Edwards on the studio presentation sequence. Eric Carney, a founder of the company, recalled that they came on right as the Comic-Con teaser was being completed.

"Gareth was a bit apprehensive about the whole thing, saying he really didn't need it," says Carney. "But through the process of making the Hawaii sequence from the film, I think he fell in love with it."

LEFT TOP, MIDDLE, AND BOTTOM "No one can draw Godzilla as well as Matt," says Edwards. These three illustrations were created by Allsopp for a possible *Godzilla* crew T-shirt. OPPOSITE This Godzilla maquette was created as the production was close to beginning filming.

"When they delivered this, I was holding it in my hands and thinking, 'Wow.' It was the first time I really got to see Godzilla. You don't really have baby photos when you're a proud parent of a movie like this, but you do get maquettes." —GARETH EDWARDS

PREVIZ IS LIKE ANY FORM OF COMPUTER GRAPHICS [CG] animation in which 3-D sets and characters are created and animated. But it's a conceptual process, so images are lower-resolution, the work varying from "down and dirty" shots to detailed sequences. "We think previz is more valuable when you put more detail into it," Eric Carney explains. "For *Godzilla*, we were able to put in a lot of detail. If, say, there's a crater and Gareth wants it smoky, we'd get smoke and atmospheric material to get it close to what he wants. He can show that to others and everyone has a common basis to work from."

"IT'S ALL ABOUT TRYING IDEAS AND PUTTING IT TOGETHER IN A SCENE TO SEE IF IT'LL WORK."

The Third Floor started with the script and Allsopp's storyboards, what Carney calls "inspirational sketches of the mood of a scene or a beat." From there, they developed all the "connective tissue" that fleshed out a static image into 3-D animation. "We worked a lot with Matt," Carney says. "We often took his storyboards and put them into the Avid [digital editing machine] and started cutting them into a sequence where we didn't have any information or know what it was. The first iteration was a little bit of storyboards and a lot of text explaining what was going on. From there we started filling in all those pieces."

MPC, which also prevized sequences, provided The Third Floor with the CG Godzilla they developed for the teaser. "We had to down-res him because usually those kinds of assets are way too heavy for us," Carney added. "We try to keep things 'light,' not too high-resolution, because we want to move through shots very quickly—we're trying to pump out a big volume of material in a short amount of time. And more than half of what we're going to do ends up on the cutting room floor. It's all about trying ideas and putting it together in a scene to see if it'll work. It becomes a discovery process."

The Third Floor's development started with research on Google Maps to create a 3-D model of San Francisco, including the Bay and Marin headlands, for a shot of Godzilla emerging by the Golden Gate Bridge. "We read the script and saw storyboards, so we knew, roughly, what the action was going to be and what we needed to build in 3-D," Carney says. "We needed to build the bridge, the water; we needed naval vessels. We needed a school bus and a driver and kids on the bus. We needed tanks, soldiers, police cars. Obviously, we needed Godzilla. It's like a script breakdown—what are all the pieces we need to create? And we have a large library of digital models we've already created, and we pull from that, buy it, or build it ourselves."

ABOVE Concept art imagines Godzilla over Alcatraz Island in San Francisco Bay. "There was, at one point, a sequence in the film where they were going to put the bomb on Alcatraz," says Edwards. "It felt a bit unrealistic because the nuclear fallout, no matter what happened, is pretty much going to be bad news for San Francisco. But I still love the idea of images you recognize from World War II movies and this insane juxtaposition with giant creatures." OPPOSITE Matt Allsopp storyboard art (top) forms the basis for a 3-D previz sequence (bottom). The images illustrate

PRIMAL SOUNDS 原始の叫び

SOUND DESIGNER ERIK AADAHL was one of the earliest members of the *Godzilla* team—he recalls being brought on by Alex Garcia not long after Gareth Edwards signed to direct. Aadahl's renaissance man résumé ranged from Michael Bay's billion-dollar blockbuster *Transformers* movies to Terrence Malick's sublime *The Tree of Life*. Godzilla's roar alone was a two-year journey, practically encompassing the entire time it took to make the movie.

"My basic philosophy is everything you hear is as important as everything you see," he says. "Sound and hearing is such a powerful sense, and my job is to use that sense to its maximum. It begins with my collecting a palette of sounds, doing a lot of recording and finding analogs I can apply and then manipulating those sounds. It's a gut thing that involves a lot of experimentation and constant tweaking, and evolves over time. It takes months and months of play and experimentation, recording and re-recording, manipulation and re-manipulation. I think Gareth really liked the fact that I had done *The Tree of Life*, so that started the discussion and experimentation. Gareth and I had a lot of back and forth over many months, working and refining Godzilla's roar."

Aadahl hails the original Toho roar as "the most iconic and famous in cinema history." The roar fit the main criteria for an iconic sound: As soon as you hear it you instantly recognize it. "It's the sound of nature, the sound of rage, a sound of power," he says. "It's a sound that would make anyone hearing it shiver. It's incredibly visceral."

Aadahl researched that seminal roar, and expresses awe and admiration for what *Gojira* sound designer Ichiro Minawa accomplished during an era of reel-to-reel analog tape recording. But then, as now, it was the sound designer's ingenuity that really produced the memorable effect—Minawa loosened the strings of a contrabass, and then took a resin-covered leather glove and slid it across the strings. The resulting friction simulated groans and shrieks he could slow down and manipulate.

"The roar in the first *Godzilla* film has a slightly different character from some of the later iterations in the '60s and '70s that were more of a shriek," Aadahl notes. "But you can still hear the seeds that germinated from the first movie. I'm sure [Toho]

never expected their sound to become one of the most famous in movie history. I felt a real obligation to honor that and stay true to it. But I also wanted to welcome it into the new era and make something fresh and high fidelity that still resonated with that original."

Aadahl would not use any original *Godzilla* recordings, but he started with the makings of the original roar, a bass and resin-covered glove: "Oftentimes, there's this element of serendipity, sometimes you get a happy accident and go, 'Wow, that's it!' And I didn't quite feel that in my gut with the contrabass. I was getting something similar [to the original sound] and something I could manipulate to sound like Godzilla, but it didn't have the fidelity, power, and richness I wanted. So I kept playing and experimenting. I recorded a lot of creatures from the ornithological world. Eventually I found the best sound was metal friction—resonating metal with dried ice. Dried ice supercools certain types of metal, and it starts contracting and vibrating and produces this shrieking and bellowing. That became the central design element for the updated Godzilla roar."

"IT'S A SOUND THAT WOULD MAKE ANYBODY HEARING IT SHIVER. IT'S INCREDIBLY VISCERAL."

Not only would the roar continue to evolve into post-production, but there would be a variety and range of Godzilla sounds. "I think of it like I'm acting, like I'm doing a sonic performance," says Aadahl. "That becomes a reference, a road map to get the whole arc of the character. And then I start plugging in the pieces to match that performance. You don't just slap roars on top of it—I want it to be a living, breathing thing. You imagine as Godzilla moves, big bellows of air are pushing through lungs the size of aircraft hangars, and as he turns you imagine his epiglottis rumbling and thumping. It begins as improvisation, and I keep refining until it feels as natural and real and exciting as I can get; my way of gauging is if it gives me goose bumps. . . ."

THE PRESENTATION

THOMAS TULL RECALLS HIS EARLY COMIC-CON TEASER discussions with Gareth Edwards emphasized the sense of a real disaster, not a stylized movie disaster: "We wanted it to evoke a sense of loss, that pit in your stomach that translates to 'Oh my god.' Forgetting that it's our movie, when Gareth cut it together and showed it to us, to this day, as a fan, it's one of my favorite teasers of all time. I was really blown away by his use of the Oppenheimer quote, which was a really inspired choice. It was absolutely Gareth's vision."

Alex Garcia notes the teaser instantly conveyed the serious tone of this Godzilla, not the cheesy "pop love" incarnations of the monster: "That teaser trailer got the momentum going. Even the first conceptual design for that piece, before it was even rendered, gave us all goose bumps. The original 1954 *Godzilla* movie was so much about Japan, post–World War II, and the franchise had gone so far away from that. That short teaser piece harnessed that same sense of relevance in a very powerful way."

Legendary decided to show the teaser as part of a presentation to Warner Bros. before publicly unveiling it as a surprise at the 2012 Comic-Con International in San Diego. "Comic-Con is kind of home base for us," Tull explains. "And we felt that everybody was going to have a point of view about *Godzilla*, the chosen director, and what our movie was going to be. So we thought, 'Let's just show something that has the DNA of our intentions and gives people a sense of what we're trying to do. Let it speak for itself.'"

First up was the studio presentation held on a soundstage at Warner Bros.' Burbank studio. The stage was adorned with huge blown-up images

ABOVE Concept art and Godzilla maquette display for the Warner Bros. presentation.

ABOVE A concept painting captures the action as Godzilla and the winged MUTO clash at the Honolulu airport while stunned travelers look on. "The idea of this . . . was a giant aquarium," says Edwards. "This feeling like when you go to these aquariums and you see these sharks swimming around and stuff, and you feel protected, but actually you're not protected at all. And so it has that quality to it, which I really like."

of concept art, two backlit images of Godzilla stretched to the ceiling, and dramatic background sounds were played to set the mood. The Comic-Con teaser and The Third Floor previz was on the program. And in the middle of it all was Gareth Edwards, there to tell the story of the film to the assembled Warner Bros. brass.

From Legendary's perspective, it was not a problem—they were making the picture, and Gareth was their guy. "Before the presentation, Gareth was nervous, but I kept reminding him, 'This is *not* a pitch,'" Tull recalls. "A pitch means you're trying to convince somebody to do something. We had an obligation to show our partner the movie and we were doing that, but Legendary was making the movie, period. Whenever we do a big movie, even if we're financing it all ourselves, we go through this [presentation] process. When you're investing that kind of capital, you want to envelop yourself in the experience, to feel that the pages of that screenplay are going to be translated into something compelling. So, when you walked into that soundstage and the *Godzilla* presentation, it was pretty impactful, seeing forty-foot banners and hearing roars and sounds of helicopters—it really gave you the sense of being there."

Tull recalls that during the presentation Edwards emphasized a "grounded" experience that was more like a disaster

"WARNER BROS. WAS IMPRESSED AND ENTHUSIASTIC, AND BOUGHT INTO THE DIRECTOR AND HIS VISION."

movie, that it would be "science plausible" even with its giant monsters. "The idea was that the responses, dialogue, and situations should all feel real and not as if you were in a fantastical world," says Tull. "Gareth talked about getting a cast that could carry that off, one that could make you believe." Warner Bros. was impressed and enthusiastic, and bought into the director and his vision.

Edwards recalls it as "the most nerve-racking day" of his life. The next "most nerve-racking day," Edwards admitted, came a week later when he did the *Godzilla* presentation at Comic-Con. "I didn't really think about it, [and that] was the problem," he says. "I'd been working really hard and hadn't had a day off, and the day before the con was my birthday. And that night, everyone bought me drinks, and I had a hangover in the morning. I

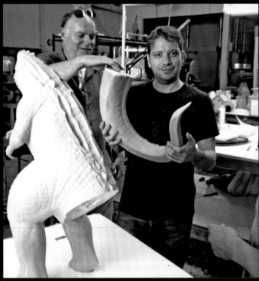

TOP Panic in the streets as a tsunami hits Honolulu in this piece of concept art. "When you're doing a Godzilla movie, [the character is] basically a walking natural disaster," says Edwards. "You can't help thinking of this type of imagery. It just taps into so many memories of terrible events." **ABOVE** The Godzilla maquette used in the presentation comes together. Gavin Bocquet (left) helped organize the Warner Bros. presentation. **OPPOSITE TOP** Frames from *Godzilla*'s teaser trailer. **OPPOSITE BOTTOM** Concept art details the iconic Vegas skyline leveled by a female MUTO. "What's great about Vegas is it's a one-stop shop for a monster," says Edwards. "You can smash up ten landmarks in one go."

thought, 'Oh god, of all the days to have a hangover! This is so stupid. I'll *never* do anything like this again!'"

In Comic-Con's world, a program slot in Hall H of the San Diego Convention Center, the biggest room with an estimated 6,500 seats, measures the upper strata of success and high expectations. "Warner Bros. Pictures and Legendary Pictures Preview Their Upcoming Line-ups" was set for Hall H on July 14, Saturday afternoon. Legendary and Warner Bros. were scheduled to present *Pacific Rim* and *Man of Steel*. The surprise *Godzilla* teaser would be slipped in after director Guillermo del Toro's *Pacific Rim* presentation.[4]

Edwards waited in the wings during the *Pacific Rim* program, and then he heard Oppenheimer's voice and the eerie temp music he had added from *2001: A Space Odyssey*. He suddenly imagined a footballer who had dreamed of taking a penalty kick in the World Cup and was now in a position to do so; looking at the ball, making the approach and then the kick, not looking up but listening for the crowd's roar that would tell whether he had scored or missed. . . .

"I was just waiting and suddenly there was this *massive*, monumental cheer that I really wasn't expecting," he says. "And when it happened I got really emotional. Suddenly I thought, 'I'm going to start *crying* or something.' It just became a bit too much. Then someone said, 'Gareth, come on stage!' And I had to go out there. I'd prepared a few things to say, and I couldn't think of anything I was supposed to say at all. I was just trying not to cry. It was so weird. I remember saying something like, 'There is nothing sci-fi about this movie,' but I didn't put in the caveat about 'apart from the giant monsters,' you know? I remember thinking, 'Hang on a minute. That didn't come out right. How could a *Godzilla* movie *not* be sci-fi?' But I wasn't thinking straight at all. I challenge anyone to go up there after showing a teaser they'd just done and not be affected by it. That was the most emotional experience I've had showing any work, ever. But there was a lot of love for it in the room. I think a lot of people had waited a long time for a studio to make this movie and, suddenly, they realized it was happening."

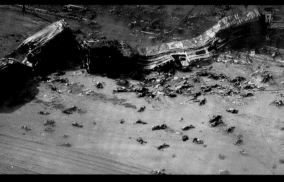

THE TRESTLE BRIDGE トレッスル橋

NOW THAT "THE DNA" OF THE SCRIPT AND VISUALS were nailed down, Legendary was officially ready to get the production rolling. "We didn't want to disappoint the fan base and have it seem in any way as if we were pursuing this branded thing to make money," Thomas Tull explains. "We certainly knew we had the right director, and once we had the right story and got Godzilla looking right—and not looking as a sort of strange derivative—it felt like we could deliver."

The production would be based at the Canadian Motion Picture Park (CMPP) in Burnaby, outside Vancouver. "A movie, in my opinion, is like a start-up company," Tull says. "There are so many details that go into it, and it all starts with people who are amazing at their jobs." He singled out a core group that included Legendary executive Alex Garcia, who was a mainstay at the Vancouver production HQ; producer Mary Parent; Legendary executive Ty Warren, who focused on production and logistics; and executive producer Patty Whitcher, who came onto the production from *The Avengers*. From there, it was about surrounding Edwards with a "first-class team" of production heads. Tull recalls initial concerns among the more established filmmakers about whether Gareth Edwards was up to the challenge: "Every single time we put a veteran in the room with Gareth, they'd sort of confide, 'Wow, this is a big step. Are you sure?' Then they'd come out, 'Where do I sign?'"

A case in point was Jim Rygiel, a three-time Oscar®-winner for his supervisorial work on *The Lord of the Rings* trilogy, who helmed the visual effects effort. "I got a call, and they told me it was *Godzilla*," he recalls. "The director did this movie called *Monsters*, right? So, I rented *Monsters* and watched it. Wow, that was pretty cool. So, then I met with Gareth, and he showed me the Comic-Con piece and I was like, 'How do I get on? Where do I sign up?' It was such a great piece. You saw the destruction and smoke billowing, and then you see Godzilla's fins move and see him rise out of the smoke. It was a fantastic shot. That sold me. I thought, 'If this is any indication of where this thing is going, it's going to be great.'"

But Edwards couldn't shake a sense of foreboding: "Never having done [a big Hollywood] film, I'd hear these horror stories of going all the way to the day of filming and someone pulls the plug and it doesn't happen. I spent the whole time in pre-production conscious that this might all be a fantasy of mine that could stop, suddenly, at any moment. Even the crew joked about it!"

The trestle bridge sequence was a barometer of Edwards' anxiety and a turning point. The story idea had emerged that, in an effort to stop the monsters, the military would deliver nuclear missiles from Nevada to San Francisco, and a train seemed the logical conveyance.

ABOVE Aaron Taylor-Johnson is ready for action in this still from the final film. BELOW The trestle bridge sequence was one of the early creative breakthroughs. In this concept painting, the looming female MUTO dwarfs the combat-ready soldiers caught on the bridge. OPPOSITE More trestle bridge sequence concept art. "Because the trestle bridge sequence in the script came with visuals, it proved the point—look how *cool* this is," screenwriter Borenstein notes.

"Ford wants to get back to his home and family in the Bay Area, and the only way to get there is to hitch a ride on this train bearing weapons of mass destruction," Borenstein says. "I remember very well the day we came up with that basic idea. We were in misery, trying to figure it out, and then there was a piercing kind of moment: 'Wow, this could be in the conversation for best sequence in the movie.' When Matt came back with coolly conceived storyboards it was, 'Okay. That's the sequence.'"

The trestle bridge sequence fit into Ford's journey story, with fate linking him to a MUTO emerging from a nuclear waste site, the creature naturally attracted to the nuclear weapons. The idea further dovetailed with an old photo Edwards had seen of Japanese soldiers, bayonets drawn, charging over a bridge in a hazy atmosphere. He couldn't shake the image, which grew into an idea of soldiers going into battle in the fog. "I knew I wanted to do a scene at some point of people running into the fog and not being able to see the creature," he says. "It was born out of this idea of a train having to cross the bridge and you can't see the other side, but we know the creature is nearby. I wanted to create a suspenseful sequence, but what was on the page didn't sound too great. It's a group decision, and we had to bring the budget down, so everyone felt 'trestle bridge' was going to go. I was thinking, 'Oh, god, I hope they don't cut this out!' Five pages of someone walking across a bridge seemed hard to defend. But when you've got a monster that's hundreds of feet tall, the obvious place to go is to have it smash things up and have people running and screaming. That gets you ten minutes of good filmmaking and then you're kind of stuck. I felt that to make this film work better we needed to build to those moments. There's a great film called *Zulu* with Michael Caine and it's about a battle, but the battle doesn't come until the end of the movie. For about an hour there's this intense buildup, knowing the enemy is coming and you're screwed. By the time you get to the battle, it's so much more powerful because you've been building up to it. I really wanted to do something like that, to milk the anticipation of the creature coming."

"I KNEW I WANTED TO DO A SCENE AT SOME POINT OF PEOPLE RUNNING INTO THE FOG NOT BEING ABLE TO SEE THE CREATURE."

Fortunately, previz on the sequence was finished at the last moment and Edwards rushed the 3-D animation to the studio just in time. To green-light the building of a set, every department head had to sign the blueprint. Around late November to early December of 2012, the trestle bridge set was signed off, the first of an eventual ninety sets. "It felt good signing that blueprint because it

was not only in the movie, it felt like things were probably going to be okay," Edwards says.

The success of the previz led to a 360-degree turn in the director's feeling about that process. Although it was typically used to work out complex visual effects sequences, Edwards wondered, *Why not previz an entire movie?* After al animation studios like Pixar did that very thing, developing their entire story with boards and story reels, temp dialogue, and sound. As it was, there was plenty to previz on *Godzilla*—the visual effects would comprise more than half the shots in the movie. The previz would be a key reference to various department heads in particular director of photography Seamus McGarvey and camera operato Mitch Dubin. Much later, in post-production, visual effects supervisor Jim Rygiel

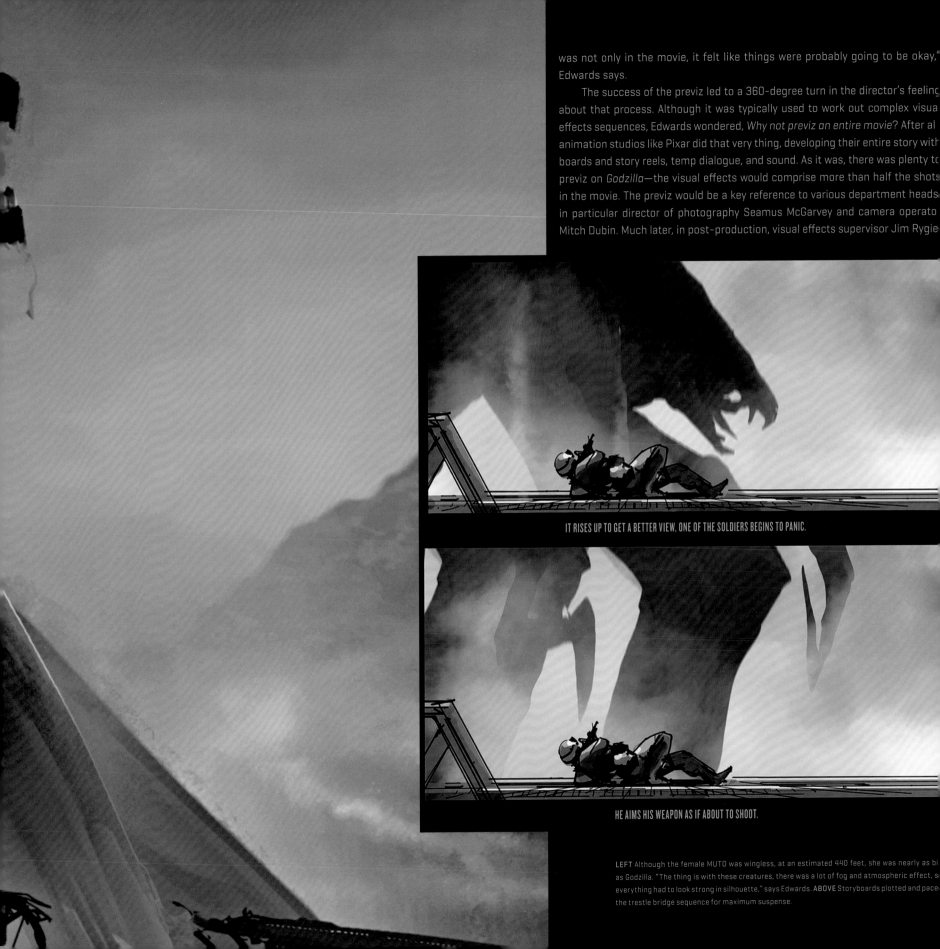

IT RISES UP TO GET A BETTER VIEW, ONE OF THE SOLDIERS BEGINS TO PANIC.

HE AIMS HIS WEAPON AS IF ABOUT TO SHOOT.

LEFT Although the female MUTO was wingless, at an estimated 440 feet, she was nearly as bi as Godzilla. "The thing is with these creatures, there was a lot of fog and atmospheric effect, s everything had to look strong in silhouette," says Edwards. ABOVE Storyboards plotted and pace the trestle bridge sequence for maximum suspense.

observed how perfectly what Edwards directed—with the camera tilting and moving on images that didn't yet exist—was in sync with the previz, while also incorporating spontaneity in the camera work. "What was great about working with Gareth was he knows visual effects," he says. "[During principal photography] you could take the previz and match

> ## WE'D LOOK AT THE PREVIZ AND WHAT THEY SHOT ON GREEN SCREEN, AND IT WAS ALMOST ONE TO ONE."

as close as you could, and from there it would sort of evolve. So each take had a slight evolvement out of the steadfast one, which is great. But [in post] we were really sticking with previz. It's sort of uncanny—we'd look at the previz and what they shot on green screen, and it was almost one to one. As the final shots got honed, the comment you'd hear a lot is, 'Make it look like the previz.' Gareth was so instrumental in that previz. I think he worked longer hours on that than the shoot. We began before the shoot, probably around November of 2012, to February or March. We were working until eleven o'clock at night sometimes, honing this previz."

OPPOSITE TOP LEFT Gareth Edwards surveys the trestle bridge location that didn't make it into the final film. "We found a fantastic trestle bridge location on Vancouver Island and we secured the right to shoot there," says art director Grant Van Der Slagt. "In the end it was too difficult, logistically, to be on a bridge 120 feet in the air with a shooting crew of 150 people. We decided to shoot everything on stage, but the location inspired us." **ABOVE** Concept art showing the aftermath of the trestle bridge's destruction. "The art department re-created this and built the whole set," says Edwards. "It was very uncanny; we would turn up everyday to a new location and it was just like standing in the concept art."

SETTING THE STAGE 舞台設定

IN ADDITION TO SETTING UP PRODUCTION offices and using soundstages at Canadian Motion Picture Park, the production utilized the facility's adjacent backlot, a former lumberyard transformed into a fourteen-acre New York set for Warner Bros. and Legendary's superhero epic, *Watchmen*.[5] The set had since fallen into disrepair, but would be made over into the streets of San Francisco. "The *Watchmen* set was basically three sets with two main intersections, and each was about 200 feet," art director Grant Van Der Slagt explains. "We used the length of one street from one intersection to the next, and we dressed the second floor with awnings, and above that visual effects continued our set."

Van Der Slagt worked closely with production designer Owen Paterson, taking the final designs and turning them into physical sets. "Gareth always had final say, but the look of the show falls on the production designer," says Van Der Slagt. "Owen and I had a whole team behind us—3-D artists and set designers, other art directors, the construction team, prop master, and the set decoration team. We didn't go for a stylized look; most of our sets were known pieces of architecture."

"One of Gareth's interesting takes on this genre is interweaving the hero's story with the excitement and terror of these huge creatures," Paterson explains. "It's as if you were standing in the long grass in Africa and watching a rhino feed— and suddenly it charges you. It's just going where it wants to go and you're in the way. I think that's the way Gareth wants us to witness these fantastic creatures."

Set decorator Elizabeth Wilcox was hired by Paterson, who was concerned, Wilcox recalls that "'there was no fabric in the movie,' that it might not be pretty enough for me. I said, 'I don't have to do drapes.'" Wilcox soon discovered that there were only a few 'character sets' in the film, but they were vital to the audience's understanding of key characters. One of the few was Ford's home in Oakland, across the Bay from San Francisco, which was actually a Vancouver house the production rented, stripped of furniture, and dressed to reflect the Brodys' family life.

It was all a logistical challenge, Wilcox notes. After she made a breakdown of the script, what concerned her at the outset was an early sequence set in the

ABOVE Shooting on the Chinatown set. "Gareth likes that feeling that this is happening for real," director of photography Seamus McGarvey recalls of filming. **RIGHT** Concept art of a lone soldier at the battered gate into San Francisco's Chinatown. "I like the idea of a gateway into where the creatures are, like it's the gateway to hell," says Edwards.

control room of the Janjira nuclear facility in Japan, circa 1999. "I knew it would take a long time to build all the blinking lights and control units and get all the wiring done," she says. "Grant made a timeline, a schedule, and a plan was in place."

As the physical sets were being planned, the official production art department was also developing creature design ideas with the director. The MUTO design included its cocoon-like spore nests; the first laid in a carcass in a Philippine mine, the second in the wreckage of San Francisco's Chinatown. "Gareth discussed having a bio-luminescence, that the MUTO gives off an electromagnetic pulse that shuts down electronic equipment and, in some cases, the spores react to that with a light burst of energy," Van Der Slagt explains. "We looked to all sorts of things for inspiration, such as sea creatures and insects and how animals lay eggs. I'm sure we had three or four dozen designs until we settled on the one Owen and Gareth were both happy with."

The Chinatown MUTO spore set became "a fairly significant build," van der Slagt explains. The soundstage itself was about 280 feet long by 110 feet wide—taking out room for fire lanes, the final set was about 200 feet long by 80 feet wide. As big as it was, digital effects would extend it farther. The construction crew built a plywood floor and sprayed a concrete product over it that they could sculpt to create the terrain. The set also included a tanker truck that had tipped over and fallen into the hole.

"Things like an aircraft carrier or the Golden Gate Bridge are wonderful toys, in a sense, for Godzilla," says Paterson. "We're like ants in the way of these creatures. They're not really conscious of us, except when we annoy them when we shoot rockets or fire guns at them."

"THINGS LIKE AN AIRCRAFT CARRIER OR THE GOLDEN GATE BRIDGE ARE WONDERFUL TOYS, IN A SENSE, FOR GODZILLA."

The backlot would also include such set pieces as the re-creation of the Grant Avenue gate into San Francisco's Chinatown that is also the gateway to a MUTO nest. "Our basic materials are wood, concrete, and foam if we're carving something intricate," Van Der Slagt explains. "We begin the design process by creating a three-dimensional digital version of the set on the computer. After the designs are finalized by Owen and approved by Gareth, they are broken down into smaller digital components and sent to a shop to be accurately cut full-size by a 5-axis CNC [Computer Numerical Control] router. After a few days we receive foam pieces that are then laid over a steel support structure by our construction team. There was a beautiful silhouette Gareth wanted of the MUTO spore burning and the actors making their way through the fog—[and] suddenly the gates are revealed. We built huge sets out of foam using this CNC process—for example, a twenty-foot-by-eighty-foot portion of a rib cage carcass for a scene in a mine in the Philippines [where the MUTO lays its spore] was CNC, cut entirely of foam, assembled on stage, and finessed by our sculpting team."

Matt Allsopp relocated to Vancouver in his capacity as an MPC conceptual artist, but actually worked in the main production office with Edwards, continuing their close working relationship. He now felt that illustrating storyboards had made him a better storyteller: "It wasn't about every second, but picking out key points, with strong silhouettes, compositions, and atmosphere that would be a great starting point—kind of the blueprint—for the previz. Gareth would talk about cameras and camera angles and how to frame things. You can create an image that's a few brushstrokes, and you like it, but when you give it to someone who has to make it 3-D, to turn that concept art into reality, then it's, 'How does this work?'"

Allsopp kept boarding, but also continued on the other path, designing creatures. Guillaume Rocheron estimated it took seven to eight months just to define Godzilla's skeleton, muscle structure, scales, and fins. It was, as Allsopp noted, a case of "How does it work?"

"We'd use the concept art to identify, 'Okay, he has these big fins on his back, but how do they grow through the skin?'" Rocheron says. "It was about adding those details and integrating the intention of the artwork and sculpt to make it look alive."

Not only was Godzilla unlike anything in nature, there were two competing aesthetics—the man in a suit versus the freedom to create realistic animal movements in CG, as with the digital dinosaurs of the *Jurassic Park* movies. "We spent a huge amount of time studying how Godzilla would move," Rocheron

ABOVE LEFT Concept art for the MUTO spore or cocoon. "The idea is that there's a creature completely folded up in here so smoothly that it just feels like one big egg or cocoon," says Edwards, "but when it opened up, you could see how the limbs were tucked in together." OPPOSITE TOP In this shot from the final film, the remains of an ancient monster are discovered in a mine in the Philippines. OPPOSITE BOTTOM The physical Philippine mine set. "We reused this set at the end of the movie, when they find the bomb in the nest," says Edwards. "It felt appropriate, because I wanted it to feel like a reprise that mirrored the opening of the film. That if they didn't stop these things, it was going to go full circle."

MAIN IMAGE Concept art for the MUTO nest that has been burrowed beneath the streets of Chinatown. "I love my silhouettes," says Edwards. "In a movie, you only get like two seconds or so for each shot and having a dark foreground always makes things easy to read." INSET "This pencil sketch is by a concept artist in Vancouver," says Edwards. "It's not on the computer; it's fantastic. This was the one that we kept sending to everybody to say, "Try to make it look like that."

explains. "The Toho version is a very upright reptile, and reptiles aren't like this in nature. But it's specific to Godzilla; everybody has that image of him upright, walking on two legs. He needed to feel upright and strong, but at the same time needed to feel agile. It's a fine balance because if you keep him too upright and stiff it looks too much like a man in a suit. You go too far on the dinosaur side, and the motion feels natural, but it doesn't feel like Godzilla."

Thomas Tull notes that as a kid he got "completely immersed" in watching black-and-white imagery of a man in a Godzilla suit. "But nowadays you can watch things happening across the world in high-def that look better than if you were actually standing right there," says Tull. "Technology has gotten so good that the 'wow' bar is much, much higher than it used to be. I remember when *Jurassic Park* came out and those creatures come over a hill—and there was a brontosaurus. I remember how I felt at that moment: 'Okay. There's a dinosaur!' But audiences are so used to seamless effects now

that you have to come up with things that are different and compelling. That was the challenge."

That challenge was largely taken on by MPC and Double Negative (DNeg), a London-based house specializing in environments, which had recently branched out into creature work on *John Carter*. With MPC handling the "hero" Godzilla shots, most of which were in the third-act monster battle, the divide put DNeg in charge of visual effects for the first two acts. For earlier shots where Godzilla is only glimpsed, MPC handed over its fully rendered, lit, and animated creature for DNeg to put into their shots.

For example, one of DNeg's Godzilla shots had the monster swimming underwater to an aircraft carrier, its fins visible above the waves. DNeg utilized MPC's entire Godzilla model, even though its virtual camera only glimpsed the fins cresting the surface of the CG waters. "It's actually easier for us to use the whole model," explains Ken McGaugh, DNeg's visual effects supervisor on *Godzilla*. "We

took the animation of Godzilla swimming underwater and did a simulation of what the water would do around his fins as Godzilla moves through."

"GODZILLA NEEDED TO FEEL UPRIGHT AND STRONG, BUT AT THE SAME TIME NEEDED TO FEEL AGILE."

The effects-heavy show necessitated that Jim Rygiel's team had to work closely with other departments to achieve the end result—a seamless shot integrating live-action and virtual elements. "These days we work very closely with visual effects," art director Van Der Slagt explains. "We were starting up the art

department around the same time that visual effects got going, because there is so much overlap with our worlds. In most instances we're designing an immediate set we're going to build, but we're also designing the set beyond. So, for example, the nuclear power plant was a practical location we augmented with catwalks and gantries, but we designed the entire facility, all the buildings, the cranes, the MUTO pit, and we handed that off as a digital asset that visual effects used as their guide as they continued on with the project long after we left."

The creative feedback cycle of Edwards, Max Borenstein, and Matt Allsopp was reunited in *Godzilla* pre-production. The production had begun prepping scenes while the screenwriter was on a cruise ship vacation with his girlfriend and his parents. Halfway between Puerto Vallarta and Cabo San Lucas, he recalls, Legendary called asking, "Where are you?" They had decided the draft needed more work and the only person who intimately knew the world, other than the director, was Borenstein. "It was a surreal moment—cut to mariachi music, phone rings, get on a plane," Borenstein laughs. "The script had to be done really fast, and that version was sent to the actors and got them on board."

It was during this early stage in Vancouver that Philip Strub, entertainment liaison for the Department of Defense (DOD), and Captain Russell Coons, director of the Navy Office of Information West, played a key role. The

production was looking for Navy support—it wanted to film and have access to aircraft carriers, for example—but key to Pentagon approval was the accurate depiction of military service. "From our preliminary look at the script, it appeared the military would be window dressing for engagements with the monsters," Captain Coons recalls. "For the Navy to participate, [a production] has to demonstrate our core values of honor, courage, and commitment."

"We appreciated and, frankly, wanted authenticity for all our military characters," adds Legendary's Alex Garcia. "Russ and Phil were fantastic partners. We all realized we were on the same page regarding what we aspired for the movie to be. They would tell us something and we would think, 'Okay, that makes a lot of sense.'"

Bob Ducsay, whose editorial department would be "the end of the line" for all of the production's visual materials, observes that the level of detail that went into creating *Godzilla* was truly mindboggling: "Every decision requires so much thought. It's one pixel at a time, one frame at a time, one line of dialogue at a time, one character at a time. A movie is really a magical amalgam of all these little details. It's so razor-thin, these tiny decisions made in the course of prepping the movie, shooting the movie—if you're off by one degree, that can be the difference between a great movie and a bad movie."

Edwards calls the process "relentless." It was light-years from *Monsters*, when he could simply walk onto a street and press the Record button on his

digital camera. "But with this film, we had to kind of build that street and put people in it," he says. "Suddenly, you have to decide what the street looks like, what are the people wearing? Obviously, you have heads of departments making decisions, but they're asking your preference all the time. I was answering what felt like a thousand questions a day."

Despite Edwards' lack of experience on a major production, producer Mary Parent feels the director's natural leadership and easygoing personality set the tone that would carry them through: "I came on in the early stages of pre-production, and while I was involved in overseeing all aspects of the production and the day-to-day shooting, my primary focus was to support Gareth's creative vision. In terms of characterizing the 'personality' of this production, I would say 'calm,' meaning that, despite the monumental task of mounting any film of this size, Gareth was always extremely calm and wonderful to work with. This had a trickle-down effect on the whole production."

The schedule for the Vancouver-based principal photography was to begin in March 2013 and continue through the end of June, with an additional three weeks in Hawaii. Edwards had been on the fast track since September, but went home to England for two weeks at the Christmas break. "It was like going from about a thousand miles an hour to, like, zero!" he says. "It's only then you realize how distracted you've been. To be honest, that was one of the hardest parts, going home. It's like when you're running a marathon they tell you not to stop, because you can get cramps and it can be harder to start again. In a story like *The Lord of the Rings*, halfway through their journey they don't go back to Hobbiton for Christmas! Finish the task and *then* I'll go home. It was a weird culture shock to go home and do normal things, knowing I had the hardest part ahead, which was the filming. We were six weeks from filming when I came back to L.A."

PART TWO

CONJURING

ROLE-PLAYING

WHEN ACTOR AARON TAYLOR-JOHNSON first met Gareth Edwards to discuss the role of Ford Brody, a lieutenant EOD [Explosive Ordinance Disposal Officer], they talked for six hours. "[Gareth talked about] the archetype, because something like *Godzilla* has that summer blockbuster feel," Taylor-Johnson notes. "But what is the journey for the audience, what is the cinematic vision? The way he wanted to shoot was to forget it's a blockbuster, commercial kind of thing. 'I want beautiful shots, I want great emotion.' I think he went for the right balance of sensitivity and testosterone. I've probably been more emotionally challenged in this film than in any independent drama or thriller. My character really goes through the wringer. I play a husband and father who finds it awkward to know how to do both things. And there's a relationship with him and his father that he's trying to mend. He starts to learn he'll do anything for the ones he loves—while *also* being attacked by giant monsters. But unless we can stop these monsters, there won't be a home, you know?"

> ## "I'VE PROBABLY BEEN MORE EMOTIONALLY CHALLENGED IN THIS FILM THAN IN ANY INDEPENDENT DRAMA OR THRILLER."

"My guy, Joe Brody, is a nuclear physicist," Bryan Cranston explains. "What a great name. Joe Brody. Sounds like a quarterback. In my series *Breaking Bad*, I patterned my alter ego name, Heisenberg, from physicist Werner Heisenberg. So I've kind of been circling around this physicist world. Brody sees an anomaly in sound patterns [at the nuclear facility in Japan] and the data doesn't support the prognosis that it's just an earthquake. We possibly need to shut down the nuclear plant to get to the bottom of it. And they don't want to listen to him, and when they do it's a bit too late. So he's a whistle-blower in all the good ways."

Edwards recalls having a dream list of actors for each role. He always envisioned Ken Watanabe as Dr. Serizawa, and they thought Cranston's "craggy gravitas" was perfect for Joe Brody. Edwards expected all the actors they wanted would say no—but everyone said yes. The final cast included Cranston, Watanabe, Taylor-Johnson, and David Strathairn, along with Juliette Binoche as Joe Brody's wife and Elizabeth Olsen as Ford's wife.

"It was quite embarrassing how good a cast we had," Edwards reflects. "What gives me the right to tell *them* how to act? But then you realize you're telling them about the film so they can make the right choices that will support that.

RIGHT Aaron Taylor-Johnson plays Ford Brody, seen here in the aftermath of a hugely destructive MUTO attack.

"Juliette, she's just royalty, really, so down-to-earth and brilliant at what she does. Ken is very precise—he does subtle, small gestures and he's got a million different looks in his face and keeps it very refined and pure. Bryan has a ton of experience and can hit his mark and do exactly the same thing with as much emotion [each take]. What surprised me is he's such a funny guy, I think he's the funniest guy I've ever met. We'd have these really intense scenes where Bryan would be in tears and at the end of a take you'd think he'd take a half hour to come down, but he'd crack a joke."

" THERE'S NO MAKING GODZILLA INTO A NICE GUY— THIS IS A BEAST AND YOU HAVE TO DEAL WITH IT. "

Taylor-Johnson's approach was what Edwards called a "slow build." As the actor got lost in the moment, "something magical would happen." Ford is not a gun-toting hero—he disarms weapons, after all—and stoically meets his challenges, whether rampaging monsters or his strained family relationships. It all wears on the hero, and to get the character's properly wrung-out emotional and physical demeanor, the actor would go sprinting off between takes, returning ready for camera and looking as if he had run a marathon.

One of the reasons Cranston wanted to do the film was he grew up loving Godzilla. "Godzilla didn't apologize for *anything!*" he says. "I think that's just the logic of a boy—Godzilla destroys everything in his path. There's no making Godzilla into a nice guy—this is a beast and you have to deal with it. Although there's a part of me that will always be that boy, I'm not the boy I was. So I was nicely surprised with the father-son relationship my character has with Aaron's character. It was

the component of the movie that attracted me the most. . . . I think what makes *Godzilla* different is that the whole sensibility [behind making] a movie like this has matured. It's not just about this beast and how are we going to control it, capture it, kill it. I think audiences need more, they demand more. And that includes investing in these characters, so you care about what happens to them."

David Strathairn's Admiral Stenz is in charge of the multiforce tactical operations that try to stop the monsters' march of destruc-tion. "He is also a career naval officer who comes with a particular way of thinking about solving these kinds of problems, how to protect the world under the [military] protocols he has learned and been trained under," Strathairn says. "He offers a rock and a hard place for Serizawa and Graham, his assistant science person. That creates a lot of the drama as to how we're going to deal with Godzilla. And when they find out there are no normal munitions that will bring these creatures down, what are you going to resort to? A nuclear device. That ups the ante in a lot of ways."

Strathairn notes Watanabe's talent in expressing the emotional turmoil of a man of science who feels there is a better path than killing Godzilla, but who fears the grim consequences the crisis has unleashed: "He's gotten under the skin of Stenz—Serizawa is tapping me on my consciousness of a larger construct: 'How do we deal with things like this? Can we let nature heal itself? Let's not mess with nature, let's keep this balance.' Ken has amazing focus. It was an honor working with him, really."

In addition to an actor's skill, there are manifold aspects to the exacting art of bringing a character to life: hair and makeup, costume, and cinematography among them. For costume designer Sharen Davis, the effects-filled *Godzilla* was a creative departure but, as it turned out, a welcome one. "Working with Gareth I could see the talent from *Monsters*—he was able to expand his style in this film," she says. "All of

ABOVE A voice howling in the wilderness—such is the fate of nuclear physicist Joe Brody (Bryan Cranston), who alone anticipates the primor-dial creatures about to be unleashed upon an unsuspecting world. ABOVE RIGHT Even Joe's son, Ford, initially dismisses his father's fears of impending doom.

LEFT Ford eventually joins his father on a journey into the mystery of the Japanese nuclear disaster that changed their lives. BELOW LEFT Ken Watanabe's Dr. Serizawa is in a constant state of tension. BELOW RIGHT David Strathairn's character, Admiral William Stenz, leads the military operations that must stop the monsters.

FORD HAZMAT
2014

Costumes Designed By:
Sharen Davis

our lead actors had very small 'costume closets.' I had to conceptualize characters before the parts were cast. There were so many hazmat/containment suits that I had to take liberties with and design looks that may push what we typically have seen."

A key part of a costume designer's job is to instantly communicate a wide range of information about a character through their chosen garb, and this was particularly true on a fast-moving epic like *Godzilla*. "I'm hoping audiences will be able to identify with all our main characters within the first five minutes of their appearance," says Davis. "My approach was to give hints of their professions with functional clothing that they would use in their specified field of expertise. I decided to put very basic clothing on our lead, played by Aaron Taylor-Johnson. He is a young Navy officer who travels for his work, so I decided on jeans, leather jacket, and a handful of knit shirts—clothing you could put in a duffel bag and is workable for weeks."

"I'M HOPING AUDIENCES WILL BE ABLE TO IDENTIFY WITH ALL OUR MAIN CHARACTERS WITHIN THE FIRST FIVE MINUTES OF THEIR APPEARANCE."

Although many of the outfits created for *Godzilla* were pragmatic rather than showy, creating costumes for a large cast and a huge number of supporting players, from military troops to fleeing refugees, proved a challenge. "The costume department was the largest I have ever worked with," says Davis. "They were very organized and professional. This was a fantastic new world for me."

OPPOSITE Ford Brody's hazmat suit (left), the Janjira facility uniform (middle), and radiation suit for Dr. Serizawa (right). Every detail, down to lapels and logos, had to be planned and created. Note the costume swatches in the upper corners. CLOCKWISE FROM TOP The stellar cast included Elizabeth Olsen, who played Ford's wife, Elle Brody; Sally Hawkins as Dr. Serizawa's associate, Dr. Vivienne Graham; and Juliette Binoche as Joe Brody's wife, Sandra Brody.

THE INNER SANCTUM

THOMAS TULL WILL ALWAYS REMEMBER SHOT NUMBER ONE on the very first day of *Godzilla* filming. They were in Vancouver, on the Japan airport set, and Akira Takarada, an iconic cast member of the previous Godzilla films, including the original, was behind a counter playing a ticket taker. "I was looking around, thinking, 'I can't believe we're making *Godzilla*! How cool is that?!'" recalls Tull. "I had this giddy feeling. To me it's always awe-inspiring for us to say 'Yes' to a movie of this scale and then see hundreds of people executing it."

To director of photography Seamus McGarvey, a film on the scale of *Godzilla* consists of an "inner sanctum" crafted by many departments, an intimate space for actors where the magic of performance is meant to happen. But outside that circle, there's an outer ring of trucks and equipment and power cables. "That's scary; I always get frightened when I approach a set," McGarvey says. "Look at what they're spending and the hundreds and hundreds of people working on something! It's a big responsibility. What I love is to forget that stuff and concentrate on what an audience will see through my lens. That's my only responsibility, really."

The producers gave the camera and lighting departments plenty of prep time, vital for a film with so many locations and complex set pieces. McGarvey worked with production designer Owen Paterson to make sure their cameras and lights would function properly on the various sets. He also consulted with visual effects supervisor Jim Rygiel to make sure the live-action photography would blend with the eventual virtual photography and digital imagery.

McGarvey could reference the previz on set but was happy the director was flexible during filming. "No amount of previz can [predict] what happens when actors start improvising," he says. "The beautiful thing about this film was Gareth was open to the possibilities of what happens in rehearsal the morning of the shoot. Gareth's previous film, *Monsters*, had a cinema vérité approach, and while we couldn't do that entirely, we were able to be more elastic and open to those lovely accidents that happen on set. That was a

OPPOSITE LEFT Taylor-Johnson in a Honolulu airport scene with a surprise cameo appearance by actor Akira Takarada, a veteran of the original *Gojira* and other classic Godzilla films. **OPPOSITE RIGHT** Gareth Edwards lines up a shot on location as cast members look on. **TOP LEFT** Edwards and Taylor-Johnson during a break in the action. **TOP RIGHT** An evacuation scene is filmed with Vancouver standing in for San Francisco. **LEFT** A crowd panics in this live-action footage for the Honolulu tsunami sequence. "It was the last day of filming, and it was kind of a relief to hit the end of a marathon," says Edwards. "We got to close a massive street and have thousands of people run down it."

necessity in order to preserve Gareth's stylistic approach. He wanted this immersive feeling, an enhanced naturalism. This film has its feet on the ground. As a result, the audience is going to be participants, slingshot, if that's the right word, into the fantastical scenarios. To that end, we had to be alive with the camera."

"The shots aren't written in stone," adds camera operator Mitch Dubin. "Everybody shows up at call time, you get the script pages and know what you're filming. You rehearse with the actors and see what they do. You have to use your eyes and imagination, and be receptive to what is there. It's not planned out weeks or months in advance. Basically, it's planned and shot on the day."

"SOMETHING HAPPENS WHEN 'ACTION' IS CALLED AND SUDDENLY A SET BECOMES THIS SORT OF SACRED ZONE."

The production shot digital, using the ARRI ALEXA Plus, McGarvey's camera of choice and the one he used on *The Avengers*. At the very end of production, the final film would be color timed using a process known as digital intermediate, or DI. McGarvey, who would supervise the DI, found it a godsend, particularly given the aesthetic decision to film in heavy atmospherics of fog and smoke—even in darkness, when a MUTO knocks out power and light at nighttime. "I've shot thirty movies on celluloid and never thought I'd say it, but I really love shooting on digital, particularly on a film like this that required low levels of light," he says. "Digital really comes into its own in that realm, the darkness. I've lit this in a way I could not have lit on regular film. I just took it to the velvety lower dimensions of darkness and that was really exciting. I remember looking at the DIT, the digital intermediate technician on set, and going, 'Are you sure this is okay? It looks pretty dark to me.' And he said, 'No, no, there's plenty there in the raw and you can pull that out.' I find that very exciting. It's not narrowing our scope as cinematographers, it's *expanding* it, this new digital world we're going into."

In the course of the shoot, the cinematographic team became intimately familiar with the actors' faces and physical mannerisms. McGarvey had to be alert to capture the unexpected moments of performance from Aaron Taylor-Johnson. Likewise, Ken Watanabe had a psychological presence and range of expressions that led the camera to go in close on him. "I think Ken Watanabe is the most mesmerizing actor I've ever photographed in terms of what he does when the camera is on him," says McGarvey. "Something happens when 'Action' is called and suddenly a set becomes this sort of sacred zone. When you've got someone like Ken who knows that and respects and harnesses it, you just get electric stuff happening.

OPPOSITE PAGE Behind-the-scenes breakdown of sequence where an exhausted Ford Brody is rescued from the San Francisco Bay during what Bryan Cranston calls "the monster bloodbath." Mitch Dubin can be seen operating the camera. **TOP** A mechanical, articulated version of the monorail car that comes under MUTO attack is filmed on a soundstage. **ABOVE** Taylor-Johnson rescues a boy—and hence, for dear life—during the MUTO's monorail attack.

There is a kind of unspoken contract certain actors have with the camera and the lenses—it's almost alchemical, something happens in the air between their face and the glass of the lens. Not overstating the fact, it's a very magical thing to witness."

Dubin referred to himself as "the director's right-hand guy." As the one looking through the lens, he was "protecting the frame, and, in essence, protecting the story," he says. "You're telling the emotional content, the perspective, and the idea of each shot. As a camera operator, when you work with really strong directors they have to be insistent with their vision. Gareth is one of those directors."

Although they shot digitally, Dubin notes that throughout the film they used original Panavision anamorphic lenses from the '50s and '60s. The only difference between shooting digitally in anamorphic—a process where the image is squeezed during filming and un-squeezed to wide-screen dimensions when projected—was their camera was squeezing images onto a film chip, not a frame of celluloid.

"There's no such thing as a digital lens," says Dubin. "The process of gathering light and projecting it will always be analog. The only difference is the older anamorphic lenses, in effect, degrade the image a little bit. I think one of the problems with digital, and why film looks so beautiful, is you feel a little removed as an audience member, because everything looks so sharp and crisp, and depth of field is too real, you're too present. You don't feel like you're watching a story; you're just reminded of reality. The concept of using these older lenses was just to soften up the digital harshness a bit, to give a sense of cinematic reality as opposed to documentary reality. Celluloid has a grain structure, and the grain moves because it's a chemical process."

Godzilla, as with any visual effects extravaganza, had those two cinematographic realities—the live-action camera and the virtual camera—and while it might seem obvious to have both in sync, Edwards notes a peculiar aspect of modern effects movies: "Some of those films have schizophrenic personalities. There's the regular part of the film and, suddenly, there's the CGI part where the camera can fly around and do crazy things that it's not doing in the rest of the movie. I felt it was important that in computer graphics we would do what we were doing in the rest of the movie. The camera was never somewhere it couldn't be, there was always a reason for how we got that shot. And we couldn't have 'suicidal shots,' anything that destroys the camera, because that means we wouldn't have gotten that footage. It sounds like silly little rules, but I think they will make the effects feel more believable. I just get frustrated seeing the CGI parts of movies doing things that cameras can't do. It never makes me go, 'That's amazing!' It makes me think, 'Oh, god, we're in the computer game again.'"

OPPOSITE TOP A helicopter arrives in the aftermath of the MUTO's destruction of the trestle bridge. OPPOSITE BOTTOM Green screen setup for a Golden Gate Bridge scene. Despite its ambitious visual effects agenda, the production used green screens sparingly. TOP The director exhorts his actors for a green screen scene, while military technical advisor James Dever (left) looks on. Note the seemingly haphazard rubble that was meticulously designed by the art department and executed by construction, set decoration, and other departments. LEFT On location in Hawaii, Edwards sets up the idyllic, pre-atomic test Bikini Atoll scene.

CONTROL ROOM コントロール・ルーム

IT'S 1999 AND THE JANJIRA NUCLEAR POWER PLANT in Janjira City is about to go into crisis mode as a nuclear meltdown appears imminent.

The plant's control room was the dramatic heart of this early sequence. The production filmed there for only two or three days, set decorator Elizabeth Wilcox recalls, but it had taken *months* to get the set ready. The watchword had been accuracy, with a consultant walking the production designer and art director through the procedures of an emergency nuclear plant shutdown. The challenge was everything had to be slightly dated and also faithful to the thousands of elements that comprise a nuclear facility in Japan.

There was also the balance with what needed to be conveyed dramatically. The control room was not big enough to have the usual lighting setup but required light sources from *within* the set. "This Tokyo nuclear power plant control room had very low ceilings, but Gareth wanted to have the camera whipping around at 360 degrees when it's in meltdown mode," McGarvey recalls. "Owen was wonderful, so collaborative. He allowed me to inform the choice of lighting fixtures and the way the set was built, so I could light from above with pseudo-fluorescent fixtures but also have lights changing from white to red. So Gareth had a choice of angles that could be worked very fast on the day."

> ## "THE CONTROL ROOM WAS NOT BIG ENOUGH TO HAVE THE USUAL LIGHTING SETUP BUT REQUIRED LIGHT SOURCES FROM *WITHIN* THE SET."

Japanese power plants have devices recording pressure within the nuclear reactor, and instead of buying real ones for $1,500 a pop, Wilcox had them made for $200 each. The set decorator oversaw the building of consoles, switches, knobs, and buttons, even supplying the paperwork and binders found in any workplace. Wilcox estimated three set designers worked for about two months to build the gauges and put together the panels. There was a graphics person in the art department who researched the correct Japanese titles for each instrument panel, while a whole other graphics department was

LEFT Dr. Brody monitors the crisis at the Janjira facility. BELOW The Janjira nuclear power plant control room was a daunting design challenge—everything from switches and gauges to signage and paperwork had to be created and accurately reflect a period Japanese nuclear facility. This piece of concept art set the look of the facility.

responsible for the imagery on computer screens. Everything, down to the fire bells, had to look like the facility was in Japan.

In true movie magic style, the nuclear facility was made of disparate elements stitched together. The exterior was an industrial space in the Vancouver area, a riverfront pulp and paper mill that had been closed and empty for years. An existing Vancouver water treatment facility had tunnels with stainless steel pipes and polished concrete floors the art department deemed perfect for scenes of panicked people running through the facility during the meltdown.

"THE EXTERIOR WAS AN INDUSTRIAL SPACE IN THE VANCOUVER AREA, A RIVERFRONT PULP AND PAPER MILL THAT HAD BEEN CLOSED AND EMPTY FOR YEARS."

"It was fooling the eye that we were in a real nuclear facility," Elizabeth Wilcox concludes. Wilcox adds that most sets were like the control room—quick shoots that required a lot of prep. And with ninety sets, the production was always on the move. "There were so many sets and things moved very quickly—you're here, you're there—the pace of the movie was very quick. It was pretty much a new set every day."

RIGHT The Janjira facility goes into meltdown in this evocative piece of concept art. "This is after the event, which is never a moment we see in the film," says Edwards. "It was one of those pieces of art that I thought useful for everybody."

INTO THE Q-ZONE

THE 1999 JANJIRA NUCLEAR POWER PLANT meltdown disaster changes everything for the Brody family—because of the evacuation, they don't have the chance to return to their nearby home. The facility and surrounding area is closed off behind a restricted area called the Quarantine Zone. Joe Brody suspects a cover-up: the authorities are hiding something within the "Q-Zone," and he believes the secret will be found in the floppy disk recordings he made at the plant—recordings left behind in his office at their old home. The passing years do not dim Joe's obsession, and finally, fifteen years later, Ford reluctantly agrees to join his father on a trip to their abandoned home in the Q-Zone.

"FINN SLOUGH WAS WONDERFUL; IT HAD THIS POSTAPOCALYPTIC AND SPECTRAL FEEL TO IT."

Their journey begins with a boat trip through a slough that flows past an eerie ghost town on an outer ring of the restricted area. The scene was shot in a Vancouver-area location called Finn Slough, a shantytown on a slough with wooden houses on stilts above the tidal water and a few dwellings built on a barge. It was not deserted—Finn Slough's residents allowed the production to film

RIGHT Concept art details the irradiated ruins of the town outside the Janjira facility. "I love postapocalyptic imagery," says Edwards. "And I just love the Japanese imagery. It's something foreign and alien anyway, even when it's normal looking. Janjira is a made-up city, but obviously Tokyo was the main influence for how this could look." ABOVE Years after the mysterious Janjira meltdown, the Brodys venture into the quarantined area, now known as the Q-Zone.

there—but the greens department added overgrown vines and greenery to make the weathered, unpainted homes look abandoned.

"Finn Slough was wonderful; it had this postapocalyptic and spectral feel to it, " Seamus McGarvey says. "It was tricky to shoot there because there were tidal considerations and the story required Aaron and Bryan to steal in on a little skiff. We shot it over two days when the tide was right and coincided with some beautiful light, and the special effects people added smoke. Its otherworldliness suggested a more languid photographic style as we traveled slowly on a low level to the water. It's wonderful to shoot in locations like that. The place kind of guides you

into it. You point your camera, and if you're sensitive enough, you record the place in a way that enhances or explores it in the right way."

The Brody men finally enter the ruins of their abandoned home. That interior set had already been filmed for scenes set in happier times. The Q-Zone sequence used the same set, but it was made over to look ruined and overgrown with vegetation, with art director Grant Van Der Slagt coordinating the trashing. "The set decorators went in and took out the furniture, and the construction department came in and started smashing the walls," Elizabeth Wilcox explains. "The paint department had the furniture over at their shop, aging it down. Then

the furniture was brought back in conjunction with the greens department putting in greens. On this show, all our sets were coordinated like that. We all had three days to accomplish this."

A key element of the ruined home was a happy birthday banner that remained on the wall of Joe's home office. Cranston's character would be at his desk when he looks up and sees it for the first time. "The moment of that reveal, when he sees this banner, is a big moment," Mitch Dubin notes. "We made a point of showing young Aaron making it ten years earlier. It's an emotional moment because it reminds him of how his life has changed. So you can't be too subtle about it."

Ultimately, father and son are arrested by Q-Zone guards and taken into the facility in time to see the emergence of what was festering in the pit of the quarantined nuclear facility—a gigantic, winged male MUTO.

DNeg supervisor Ken McGaugh explains the Q-Zone pit included both the virtual environment they created and an adroit use of the abandoned paper mill shooting location. "The 'Host MUTO Hatches' was our biggest sequence," McGaugh explains. "We did lots of virtual environments, creature work, and action and destruction there. They essentially shot on the real location, but used different angles. When combined with our virtual backgrounds, it made you feel like you were in different parts of the facility."

> "ULTIMATELY, FATHER AND SON ARE ARRESTED BY Q-ZONE GUARDS AND TAKEN INTO THE FACILITY IN TIME TO SEE THE EMERGENCE OF WHAT WAS FESTERING IN THE PIT OF THE QUARANTINED NUCLEAR FACILITY— A GIGANTIC, WINGED MALE MUTO."

TOP Concept art strikes a melancholy mood as father and son return to the old neighborhood, now a graveyard of bitter memories. "This is a real location," says Edwards. "The art department and the location guys would find real places that looked like they could work for us. This image is the art department sort of explaining what they planned to do before we filmed there, how they would destroy it all." **RIGHT** Ford and Joe Brody encounter a stray dog in this still from the finished film.

MAKING MONSTERS

FILMING WAS UNDERWAY WHEN GARETH EDWARDS dropped by MPC's production office in Vancouver to see a 3-D motion study of Godzilla walking by the Golden Gate Bridge. Guillaume Rocheron recalls the director's reaction: "'Oh my god! This is Godzilla!' We looked at it for like ten minutes. For Gareth it was the first time he saw the creature he had in his head. We had a 3-D Golden Gate Bridge and Godzilla walks alongside it, he looks underneath the bridge and around. Gareth loved how it felt, how Godzilla was behaving. The silhouette was Godzilla, but he was moving in a very agile way. It was also very animalistic, because we looked at a lot of references of how animals scan their environment when they're search-ing for something. It's faithful to the Toho version, but at the same time, he has a photorealism that will make him fit into a movie that comes out in 2014."

For Godzilla's fins, Rocheron pointed his design team toward oyster shells, for skin they looked at lizards and alligators, for Godzilla's teeth they referenced prehistoric T. rex teeth. But with a character hundreds of feet tall, nature was only a starting point—Rocheron notes that each of Godzilla's toenails was as big as a car: "We'd organize a texture shoot of an alligator, but if you put an alligator scale on Godzilla it doesn't look right, because an alligator is like ten to fifteen feet."

"The first stop was Weta. In terms of Godzilla, Andrew Baker, Christian Pearce, and Greg Broadmore each did over a hundred designs for the first pass. We knew we had to be true to Godzilla, but we didn't want any rules in terms of new shapes and silhouettes." —GARETH EDWARDS

"[Once the design was developed,] this was Matt Allsopp's 'Now that I know what Godzilla looks like, I'm going to draw a great image' piece of artwork." —GE

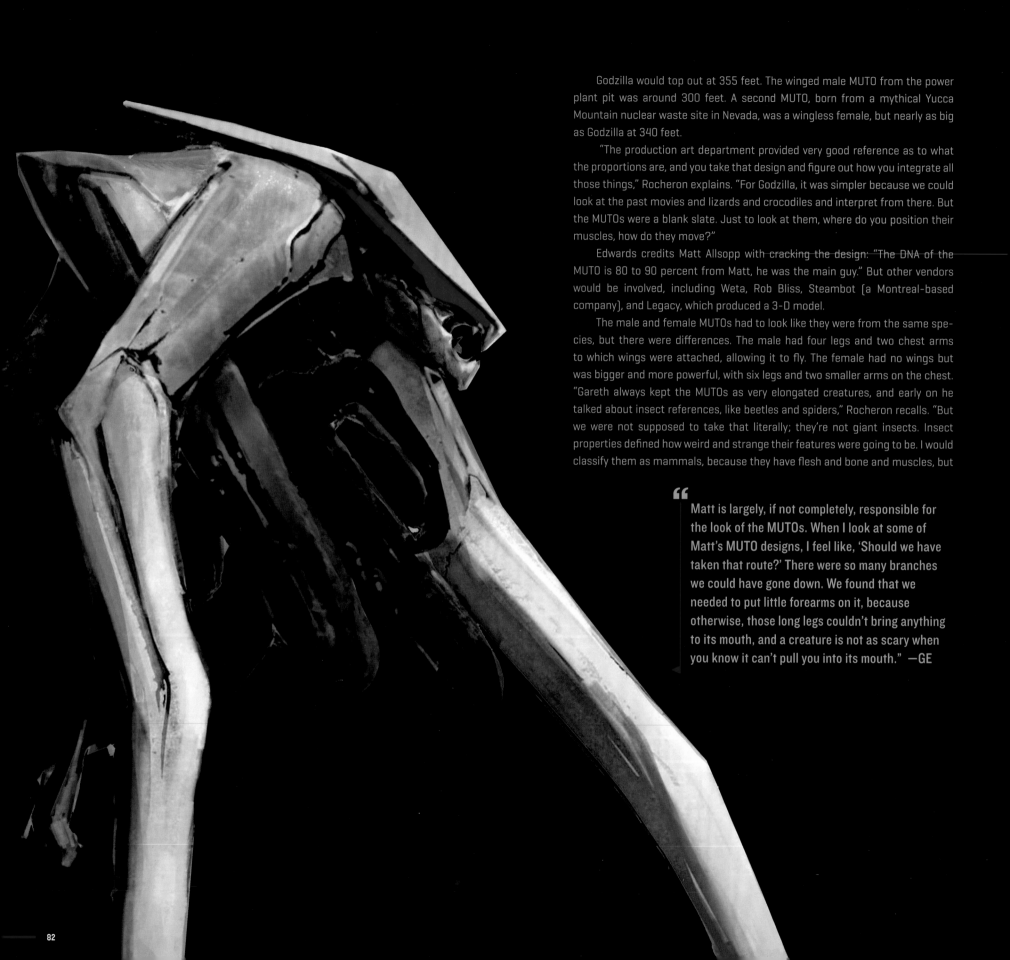

Godzilla would top out at 355 feet. The winged male MUTO from the power plant pit was around 300 feet. A second MUTO, born from a mythical Yucca Mountain nuclear waste site in Nevada, was a wingless female, but nearly as big as Godzilla at 340 feet.

"The production art department provided very good reference as to what the proportions are, and you take that design and figure out how you integrate all those things," Rocheron explains. "For Godzilla, it was simpler because we could look at the past movies and lizards and crocodiles and interpret from there. But the MUTOs were a blank slate. Just to look at them, where do you position their muscles, how do they move?"

Edwards credits Matt Allsopp with cracking the design: "The DNA of the MUTO is 80 to 90 percent from Matt, he was the main guy." But other vendors would be involved, including Weta, Rob Bliss, Steambot (a Montreal-based company), and Legacy, which produced a 3-D model.

The male and female MUTOs had to look like they were from the same species, but there were differences. The male had four legs and two chest arms to which wings were attached, allowing it to fly. The female had no wings but was bigger and more powerful, with six legs and two smaller arms on the chest. "Gareth always kept the MUTOs as very elongated creatures, and early on he talked about insect references, like beetles and spiders," Rocheron recalls. "But we were not supposed to take that literally; they're not giant insects. Insect properties defined how weird and strange their features were going to be. I would classify them as mammals, because they have flesh and bone and muscles, but

"

Matt is largely, if not completely, responsible for the look of the MUTOs. When I look at some of Matt's MUTO designs, I feel like, 'Should we have taken that route?' There were so many branches we could have gone down. We found that we needed to put little forearms on it, because otherwise, those long legs couldn't bring anything to its mouth, and a creature is not as scary when you know it can't pull you into its mouth." —GE

"One of the things we ended up saying was, 'Okay, we've got Godzilla.' So what would the fish Godzilla look like? Okay, now we're going to have the reptile Godzilla. Now we're going to have the dragon Godzilla. Just to push Godzilla into places that you wouldn't naturally go. You might get nothing from it, but [from this process] the gills might come. You might say, oh, he should have gills. He's underwater and he's got no lungs—how else does he breathe? It might make some fans turn in their graves to know that we did this, but if just one thing comes from it, it's well worth it." — GE

" Andrew Baker was probably the biggest creative influence on the look of Godzilla. I spent many nights Skyping him, seeing a live feed from his desktop as he sculpted and tweaked a 3-D version of Godzilla." —GE

"This was Christian's, and the big breakthrough here was having the eyebrow almost in line with the snout. It gives it a very noble-looking character, which is the quality of the eagle. It seemed the way to go. We wanted to combine the realism of Andrew's stuff with what Christian was doing." —GE

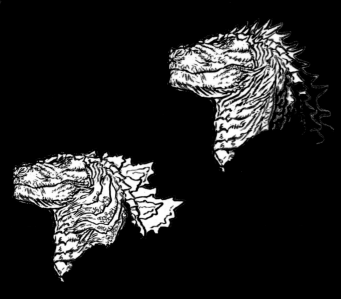

"We kept looking to three main animals—a bear, dog, and eagle. There's something noble about an eagle, and that was the breakthrough, that [the designs] should go more toward birds of prey." —GE

"
This was a breakthrough image that Matt did in regard to Godzilla's face.
MPC were clicking through some images, and it was like, 'Oh wow, yeah,
that's great, go back to that image. Let's make it look like that.'" — CE

"This is Matt's. He tweaked this as we took it to 3-D. We got real close, and this one feels like Matt pushed it to completion."   —GE

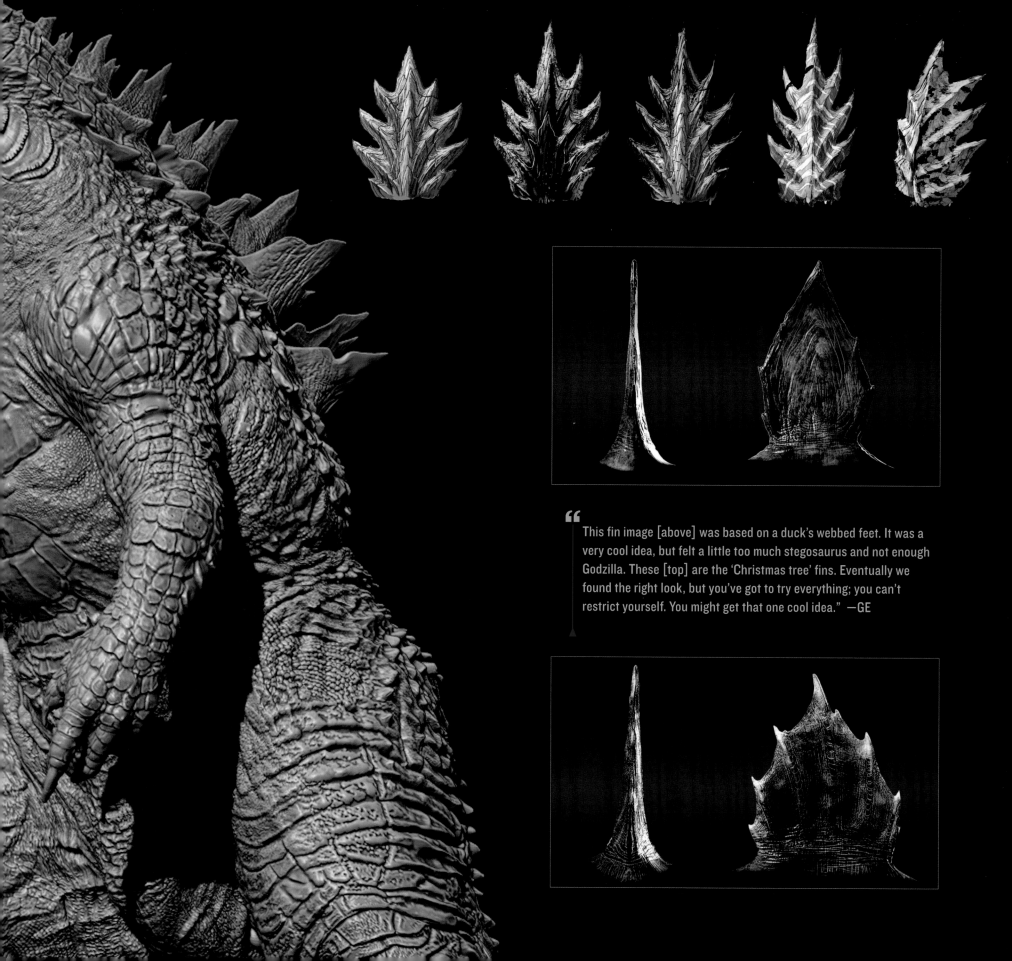

"This fin image [above] was based on a duck's webbed feet. It was a very cool idea, but felt a little too much stegosaurus and not enough Godzilla. These [top] are the 'Christmas tree' fins. Eventually we found the right look, but you've got to try everything; you can't restrict yourself. You might get that one cool idea." —GE

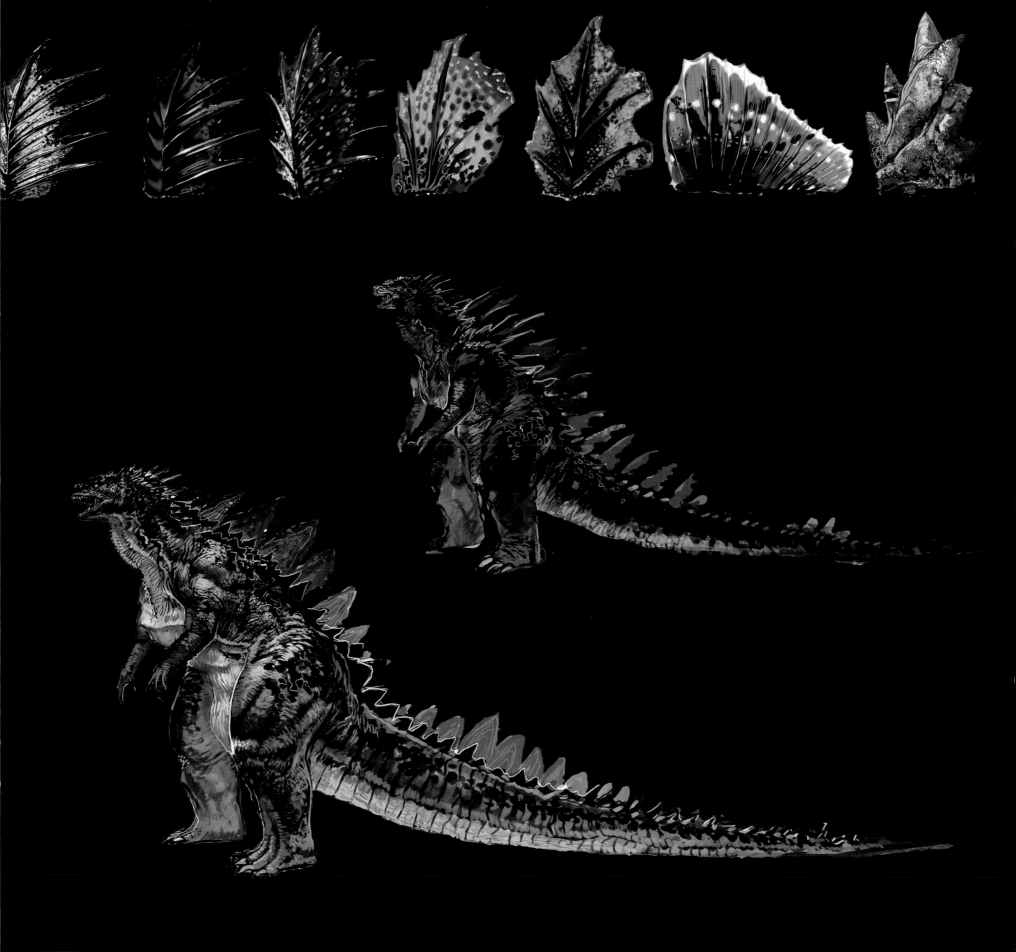

MUTO EVOLUTION

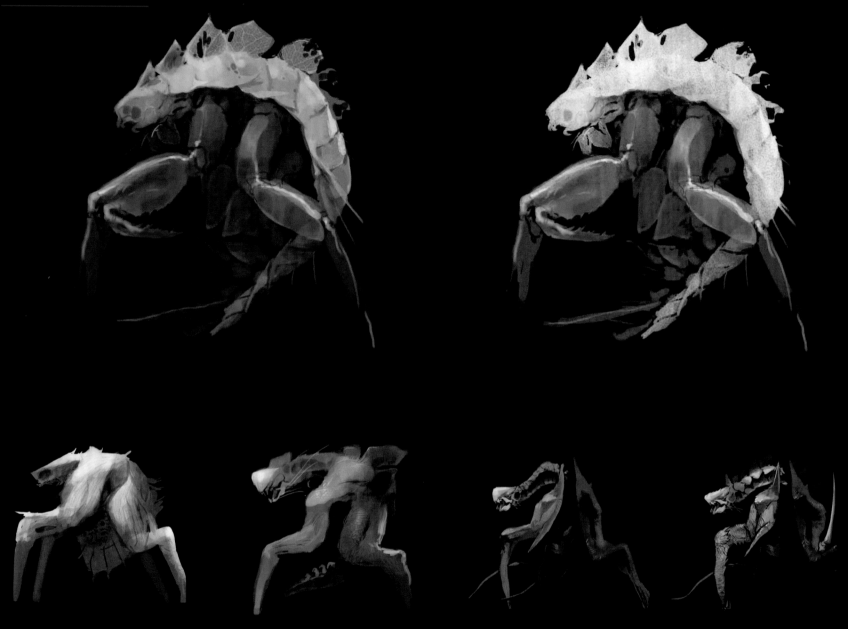

" [For the MUTOs] we were looking at the idea of insects and sea creatures and making them massive. I really liked the leg configuration on the side angle. There was something disturbing about it. For me, that became the starting point, the shape I wanted to explore." —GE

"[These early MUTO designs] felt like the skeletal part of a shark or something, but on the outside of the creature, so it has this kind of skeletal fish effect. It's funny, because if we ever did another film, I'd go through this book and use these as branching-off points for other creatures. It's a shame, because there are some nice ideas that inevitably fall by the wayside." —GE

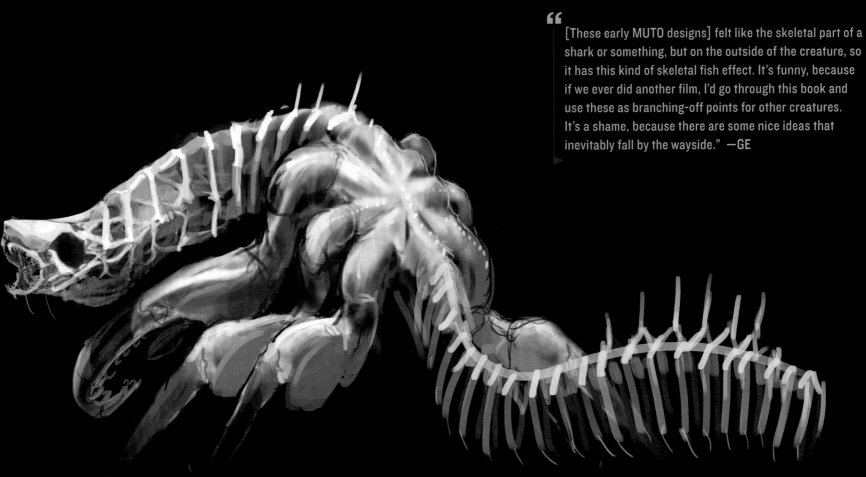

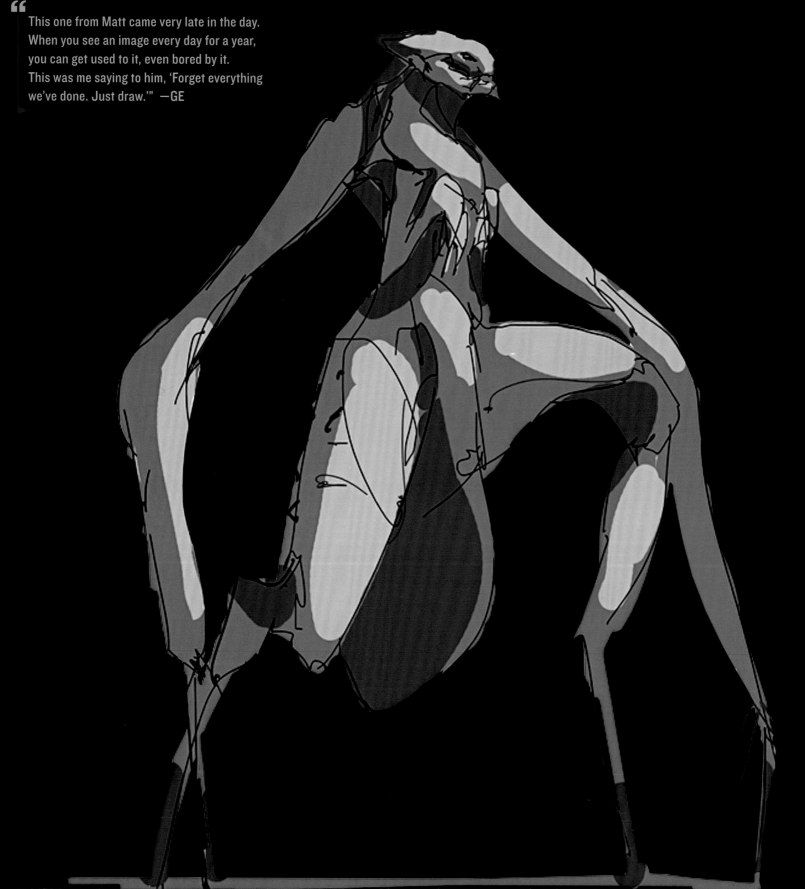

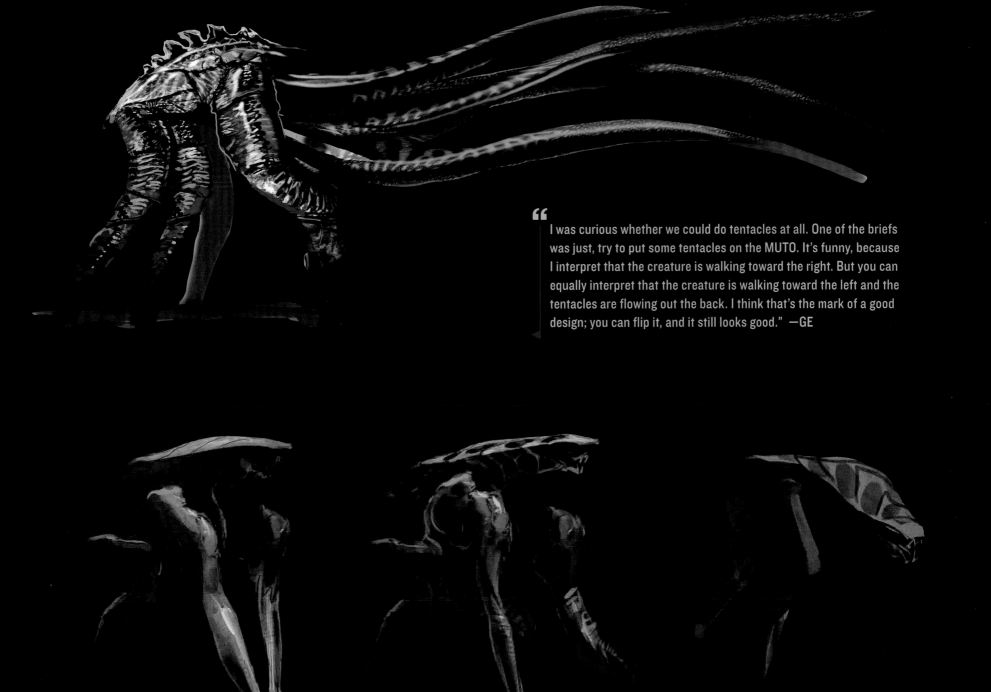

"I was curious whether we could do tentacles at all. One of the briefs was just, try to put some tentacles on the MUTO. It's funny, because I interpret that the creature is walking toward the right. But you can equally interpret that the creature is walking toward the left and the tentacles are flowing out the back. I think that's the mark of a good design; you can flip it, and it still looks good." —GE

"These are by Aaron Beck [at Weta] and are really cool. Aaron's really good at what I called stealth muscles, these angular shapes and cartilage-looking flesh. His approach of doing muscles was different and not something you would find in nature, but you felt it could be. And that inspiration was where we took the MUTO." —GE

" Legacy was doing a fantastic job making a 3-D Godzilla model and maquette, so we felt, 'Why don't you take a crack at the MUTO design as well?' Legacy designs in 3-D, and it's really like time lapsing evolution. When you pull the eyes apart you realize how real organisms evolved—suddenly, with a few brushstrokes, thousands of years of evolution go past." —GE

" This one felt like an organic version of the tripods in *War of the Worlds*. I love the long legs— there's something disturbing about a creature that can reach down [that far]. But it just felt a bit too close to *War of the Worlds*." —GE

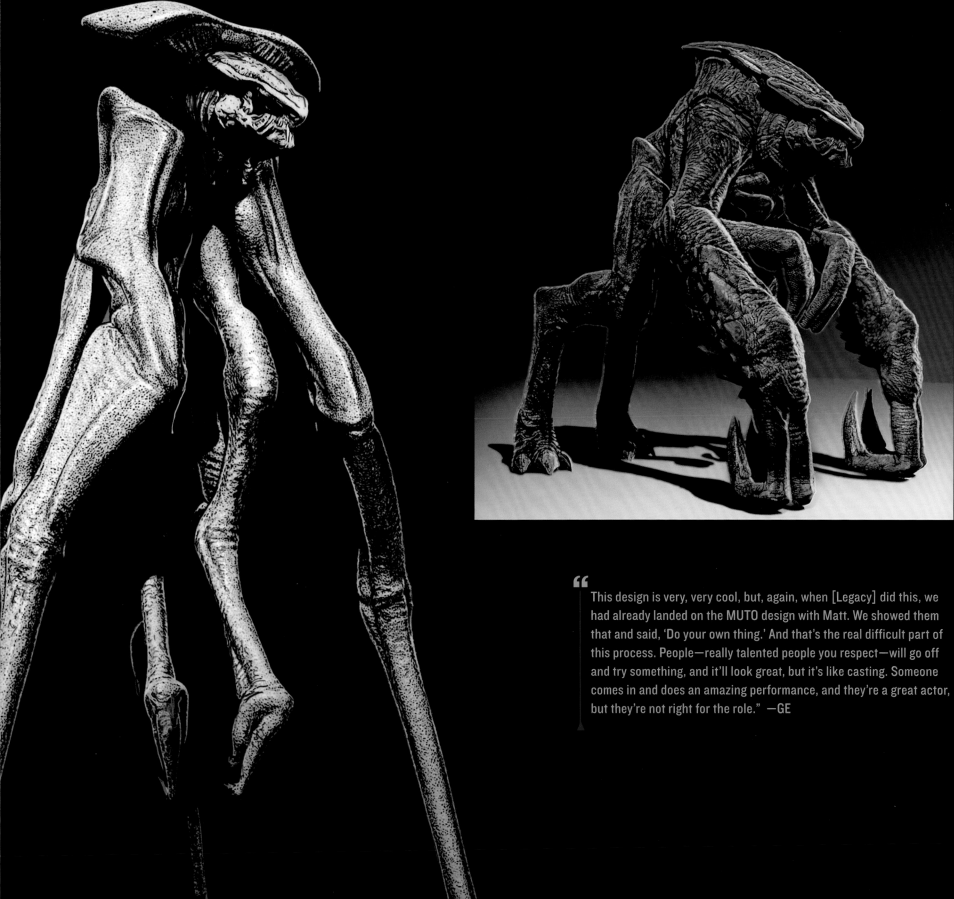

This design is very, very cool, but, again, when [Legacy] did this, we had already landed on the MUTO design with Matt. We showed them that and said, 'Do your own thing.' And that's the real difficult part of this process. People—really talented people you respect—will go off and try something, and it'll look great, but it's like casting. Someone comes in and does an amazing performance, and they're a great actor, but they're not right for the role." —GE

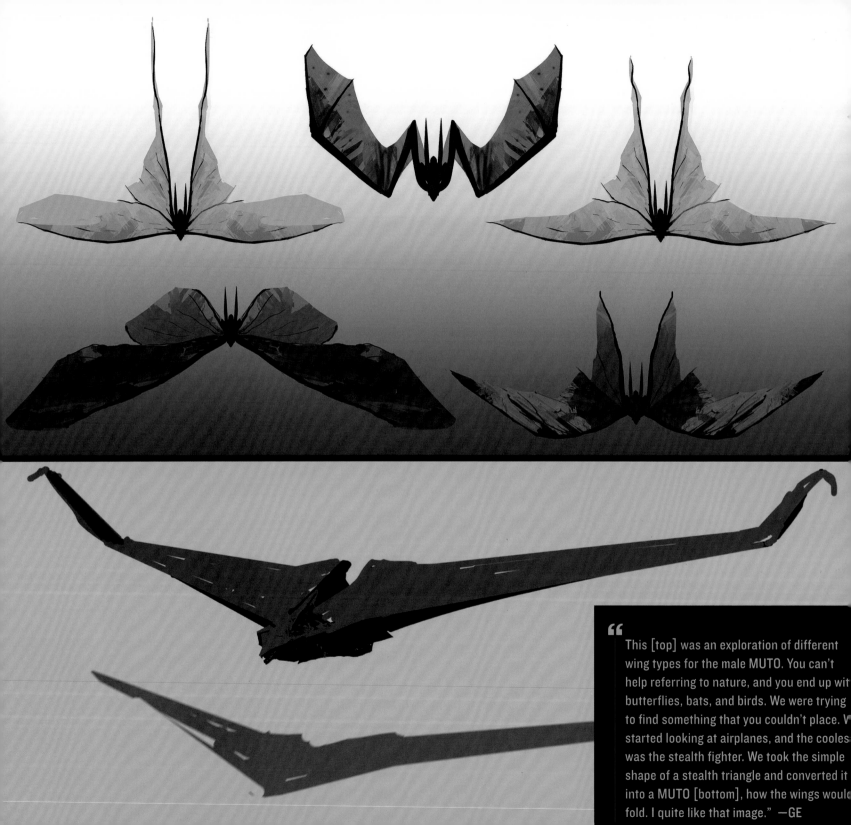

"This [top] was an exploration of different wing types for the male MUTO. You can't help referring to nature, and you end up wit butterflies, bats, and birds. We were trying to find something that you couldn't place. V started looking at airplanes, and the cooles was the stealth fighter. We took the simple shape of a stealth triangle and converted it into a MUTO [bottom], how the wings woul fold. I quite like that image." —GE

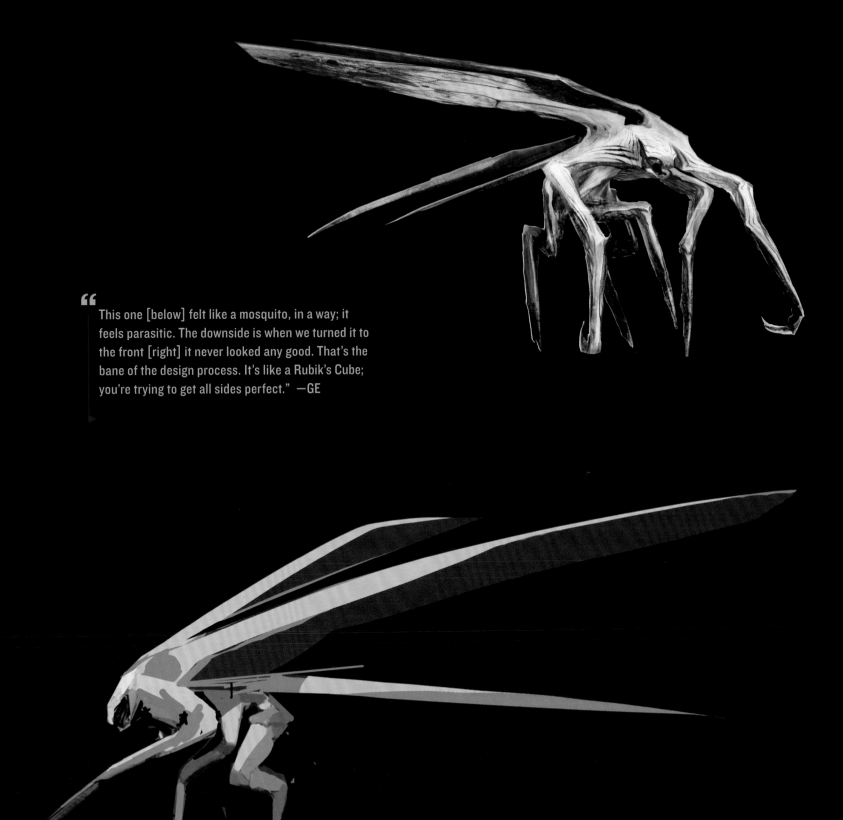

"This one [below] felt like a mosquito, in a way; it feels parasitic. The downside is when we turned it to the front [right] it never looked any good. That's the bane of the design process. It's like a Rubik's Cube; you're trying to get all sides perfect." —GE

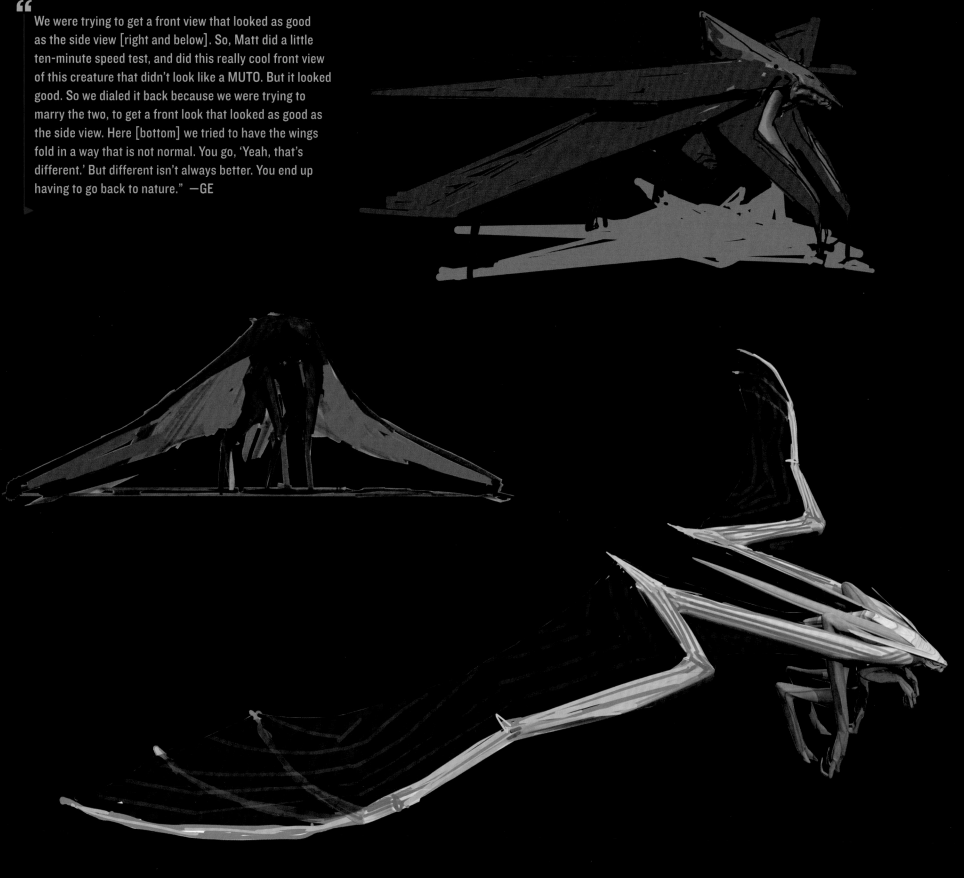

"We were trying to get a front view that looked as good as the side view [right and below]. So, Matt did a little ten-minute speed test, and did this really cool front view of this creature that didn't look like a MUTO. But it looked good. So we dialed it back because we were trying to marry the two, to get a front look that looked as good as the side view. Here [bottom] we tried to have the wings fold in a way that is not normal. You go, 'Yeah, that's different.' But different isn't always better. You end up having to go back to nature." —GE

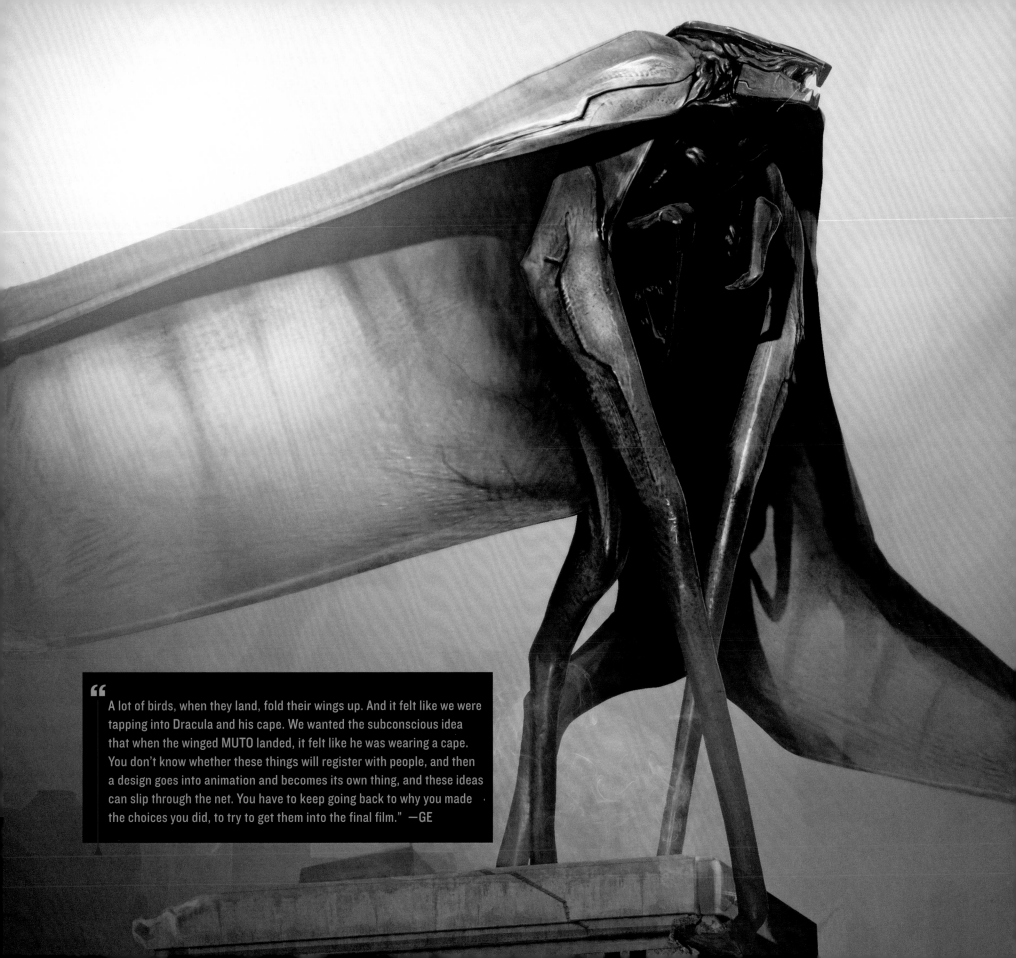

"A lot of birds, when they land, fold their wings up. And it felt like we were tapping into Dracula and his cape. We wanted the subconscious idea that when the winged MUTO landed, it felt like he was wearing a cape. You don't know whether these things will register with people, and then a design goes into animation and becomes its own thing, and these ideas can slip through the net. You have to keep going back to why you made the choices you did, to try to get them into the final film." —GE

ABOVE AND RIGHT MUTO designs take the creature to San Francisco,
the site of the climactic clash of the monsters.

PATH OF DESTRUCTION 破壊の道

BRYAN CRANSTON HAS A FEW THINGS TO SAY about his friend and co-star, the Big Guy himself: "Godzilla is unfairly blamed for a lot of troubling things. Godzilla has been a great person to work with on the set. His temperament is actually very kind and calm. He's a professional. So, when it's time to destroy a city, he'll do it, but up until then, he talks about his family a lot. You know, he's a good family guy, misses his kids. Location work does that."

Every day, when cast and crew arrived on the set, the spirit of Godzilla was there with them. "At the end, Godzilla will be the star of the film," notes Mitch Dubin.

"I think the reason monster movies are popular is because we've evolved," Gareth Edwards muses. "We once lived in caves or huts and there was always animals that could come out of the woods to kill us. Now we live in massive skyscrapers and multistory buildings, but that instinct that something is going to come kill us is still within us. Our homes and cities have become bigger and stronger so our fear of the animal becomes bigger and stronger. It seems crazy, but subconsciously it feels possible. It feels that we've had it so good and some-day soon something is going to come and put things back to where they were."

Alex Garcia notes the dichotomy of monsters represented dual aspects of nature itself. Godzilla was ultimately the force for bringing the world into bal-ance. "We humans like to think of ourselves as all-knowing and all-controlling," Garcia says. "The reality is we are fairly fragile and exist in a system where upheaval can wipe us away. The MUTOs represent the malevolent side of nature. On some level, our tampering with nature has allowed these creatures to grow

stronger. We've helped create an imbalance, and Godzilla moves in to right the balance. He is not our 'hero,' but represents something greater—he is saving us in the process of righting the balance. It's the idea that we have to provide a harmony within that balance, which is compelling."

As the monsters move through the human world, they leave destruction in their wake. For the aftermath of the MUTO damage in Hawaii, the art department created a rubble pile in front of the Hilton on Waikiki, a physical element of foreground destruction that would mesh with DNeg's CG imagery of the collapsed hotel. "It's not that the MUTO is purposely trashing the human world—things are just sort of in its path," Elizabeth Wilcox explains. "For the Hilton, we had a rubble pile to represent the hotel rooms. We had bathrooms,

headboards, beds, suitcases, toys, a teddy bear, beach towels, shoes, the personal things you'd have taken on vacation. All the rubble had to be shipped there. So when you're busy working in May on the Chinatown set in Vancouver, the aircraft carrier, and the Q-Zone, you're ordering things in Los Angeles to ship to Hawaii in July. I had a very good team in Los Angeles to help."

"Rubble pile" was the byword for the "practical" destruction. "Each rubble pile had to have its own character," Wilcox explains. "The MUTO ravaging

BELOW San Francisco digs out from the ruins of the monsters' battle. Note the ruined Bay Area Rapid Transit train system station on Market Street.

LEFT A piece of concept art (top) and two storyboard panels (middle and bottom) depict monster wreckage on Waikiki Beach. BELOW A vanquished MUTO draws awed onlookers in this early concept painting. "There was an early version of the screenplay where the MUTO got killed," says Edwards. "But what it was actually doing was cocooning and it was going to grow wings and re-hatch halfway through the film. We just felt that there were too many iterations of its life cycles, so we dropped the idea."

the nuclear facility in Japan was basically construction rubble, although we got railings and pipes and a section of a crane piece. For the San Francisco sequence, there was a Financial District and BART [Bay Area Rapid Transit] station set, so we had destroyed desks, bookcases, and vertical blinds."

"We had a team of people from the construction department that came out and laid in the bigger pieces of concrete rubble," explains Van Der Slagt, "and behind that, the set decoration team came in and put the crushed furniture and the blinds and pipes and conduit and all that kind of debris on top. And, on top of that, our scenic artists go in and put in burn marks as if there was a gas fire and things have been charred. The final step is our greens person dusts the set down with concrete dust and smaller rubble."

A major aspect of Double Negative's shots was the backgrounds and vistas of the swath of destruction. Their work ranged from digital matte paintings depicting the ruins of Caesar's Palace in Las Vegas to virtual backdrops, such as the ruined Hilton in Hawaii. For a helicopter flyover of the aftermath of a MUTO Vegas rampage, initially created as a green screen

element showing actors looking out over the devastation, the virtual backgrounds had to match the live-action camera movement and the actors' eye lines.

"THE MUTOS REPRESENT THE MALEVOLENT SIDE OF NATURE."

Although most of DNeg's destruction aftermath was driven by the early concept art, the ruins of Caesar's Palace were a rare exception. All they had to work with was a foreground element, shot during principal photography, showing an actor playing a firefighter. In the final shot, the firefighter was supposed to be gazing out at the ruins of the fabled casino. The digital matte painting was worked out in post-production cineSync sessions between the DNeg artists in London, and Edwards, Rygiel, and the visual effects team at their post-production head-quarters in Burbank. "This was 'postviz,' where we

conceptualized the casino ruins in post-production using the actual filmed footage for the shot," DNeg visual effects supervisor Ken McGaugh explains. "It was a very iterative process, the biggest problem being adding the layers and depth so you have a realistic parallax shift, that sense of objects moving in relation to each other, so it's not static."

A major challenge, McGaugh adds, was that although there are many references for the destructive aftermath of wars and natural disasters, it was a puzzle figuring out the reality of a MUTO's path of destruction. McGaugh characterizes the destruction along the Vegas Strip as resembling a violently carved trench: "We found the more we tried to rationalize how the destruction happened, the more boring it ended up looking. At the end of the day, [we went for] what made a shot look good, balanced with a gritty realism. Vegas was a good example of this, in that we weren't sure *how* a MUTO would create a big trench through the city. But it looked really good and added an epic scale to the destruction."

Meanwhile, sound designer Erik Aadahl approached the sounds of destruction like a symphony. "For destruction, I don't like noise, I don't want an audience to be pushed away—I want them pulled in," he says. "For example, for a skyscraper getting crashed into and coming down, you often find the macro in the micro. One of my favorite things is to play with Swedish crisp bread. It's very crunchy and when you put a microphone very close and gently start to crack it, you get a nice long rippling crack sound. I can take that into the computer and manipulate it, enhance it, and make it sound like the earth is splitting open. I also like using big blocks of ice that have a lot of weight and can crunch and crack. I'll send those tumbling down staircases or dump them off the roof. The nice thing about ice is it melts afterwards, there's no brick and rubble to clean up."

LEFT AND BELOW From Nevada, a female MUTO begins her trek to the West Coast in these explosive concept art pieces. "I wanted to represent something of the MUTO's journey across the U.S.," says Edwards. "The problem is you've got so little time in a movie—it feels like an entire movie could take place down in that town—but we only had time for one shot or so, so this is me trying to get it in." **OPPOSITE BOTTOM** A storyboard depicts the catastrophic aftermath of the MUTO's cross-country rampage.

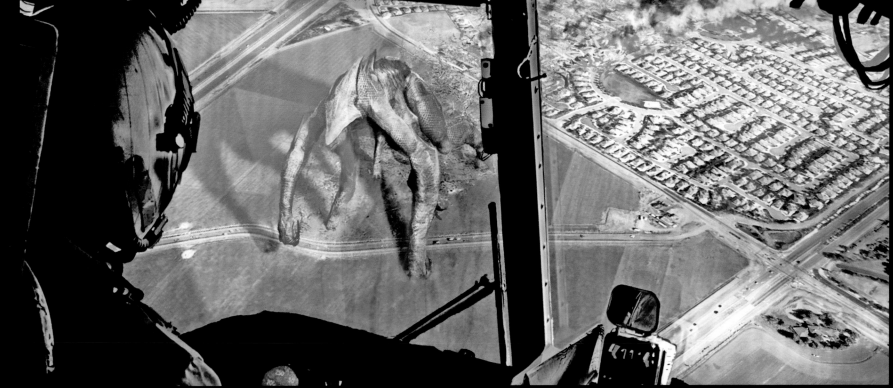

SMOKE AND SHADOW

SEAMUS MCGARVEY RECALLS THAT WHEN production designer Owen Paterson discussed the exterior backlot in Vancouver his advice was that "darkness was their friend." The old *Watchmen* set was "rickety," as McGarvey put it. In addition to practical concerns was the need to realize the director's moody aesthetic that made heavy use of smoke and shadows to both hide and reveal key elements of the film. The style was set with the seminal Comic-Con teaser that showed Godzilla emerging from clouds of dust.

"I think Gareth's style is about elliptical views of things," McGarvey muses. "I never used so much smoke; and I've never shot film as dark as this one. But Gareth loved that and encouraged me to be brave with the light. He kept trying to up the ante with each set and he'd get so excited when he achieved something that was better than he imagined. He'd say, 'Let's not be complacent, let's go even further the next time.' It's just wonderful having a director who's excited about the possibilities of cinema, as Gareth is."

The big problem with smoke and other atmospherics was it made things difficult for visual effects. "Visual effects supervisors almost universally don't want you to use smoke; they want to add it later," McGarvey explains. "But it just looks awful when it's done that way. But Jim Rygiel was very collaborative in knowing when I really needed smoke. Jim has a great cinematographic eye, and that has become an increasingly important part of my job as I take on these visual effects movies and have to make sure, with the visual effects supervisor, that we're on the same path, visually. It made it a little more difficult for him in post, but it was a cinematographic prerequisite that I was going to use smoke."

"LET'S NOT BE COMPLACENT, LET'S GO EVEN FURTHER THE NEXT TIME."

In terms of integrating a smoky live-action set with computer imagery, Rygiel already had experience from his work with director Peter Jackson on *The Lord of the Rings*: "Peter would say, 'Okay, I know we have a big green screen over there, but I want to shoot it over here and I want a lot of atmosphere and smoke in the shot.' So we did *tons* of rotoscoping." A process as old as animation itself, rotoscoping involves taking live-action footage and tracing around the elements that the filmmaker wants to keep while replacing other aspects with matte paintings and other effects.

Art director Grant Van Der Slagt adds that Edwards' knowledge of visual effects made for a nimble use of technology: "This is the first time I've ever been involved in a film where we didn't use as much green screen as I thought we would. We were in environments where Gareth and the visual effects supervisor and

RIGHT Concept art imagines the surreal effect of the giant monsters, such as this nuclear submarine dropped in the mountains. "I love this shot," says Edwards. "We struggled with trying to find a position for the submarine that didn't feel too silly, but you could still read it from a distance. This is a shot that's never in the film, they don't actually approach it from the boat, but again, things get drawn just to give it flavor."

producer would have a discussion and decide they would just rotoscope everything out of the frame. It's a laborious task, but allows more freedom when you're shooting at a location."

Alex Garcia notes that Legendary always planned to harness Edwards' knowledge and facility with visual effects: "In *Monsters*, Gareth basically did the visual effects himself and applied them in such an innovative way. Applying that technique on a much larger canvas was always something we talked about trying to do. We wanted to allow Gareth a freedom of style, rather than a process that would constrain the vision."

DNeg supervisor Ken McGaugh adds that Edwards' approach was to get as much "in-camera" as possible, using green screen only when the quality of the eventual shot would be compromised. DNeg used their in-house rotoscoping software, affectionately called "Noodles," to integrate the live-action photography with the virtual backgrounds—primarily images of destruction.

> ## "WE WANTED TO ALLOW GARETH A FREEDOM OF STYLE, RATHER THAN A PROCESS THAT WOULD CONSTRAIN HIS VISION."

"Knowing you're going to be doing that, and planning for it, gives you a lot more freedom while shooting," says McGaugh. "We'd be putting in the backgrounds, so we had to rotoscope people and objects, to pull them back in front. It's not a procedural process, but very manual, especially when you have organic shapes that are moving. It's real tedious work dealing with the fine edges, making sure the real footage isn't bleeding through those edges."

McGaugh recalls one of those proverbial "happy accidents" during the filming of the Hilton in Hawaii, when a sweeping camera move suddenly took in a flock of birds that swept in, did a dramatic loop in the middle of the frame, and then flew out of camera: "It was so perfectly timed that Gareth was just desperate to keep it, and we promised him we'd rotoscope every one of those little birds to make sure they stayed when we put all our destruction into the shot. It looked like it was planned, it was so perfectly choreographed."

The atmospherics and live-action lighting still retained the desired "photographic naturalism," McGarvey maintains: "There's the unbelievable skin of Godzilla, for instance, that they built and rendered and pushed back through a diffusion of atmosphere, of light and lightning and elliptical flashes, this incredibly spartan use of visual effects. Audiences are lathered with over-the-top visual effects, but I think they're becoming bored with that. What's nice about this film is it has high-end visual effects, but used sparingly."

There was also the conundrum of finding a lighting source when a MUTO's natural force field shut off electrical power and plunged a scene into darkness. Working with no light was one of the big challenges on *Godzilla*. To overcome it, McGarvey researched some of revered photographer Edward Steichen's misty, dreamlike imagery that looked as if it was exposed under moonlight but had in fact been shot in the daytime: "We wanted to avoid the Hollywood blue backlight feeling you get, and go for something more nocturnal."

McGarvey worked with gaffer Stuart Haggerty to design huge "soft boxes" to provide a light source emulating the "cinematographic darkness" the director of photography hoped for.

The huge array of lights, when lifted up on a 160-foot crane, looked like "the biggest stadium light you ever saw," McGarvey says, estimating the setup was 260 lamps and 260,000 kilowatts per light box. They had two, with Haggerty christening one "Big Seamus" and the other "Wee Seamus." Diffusion materials were then built over those blinding light boxes. "It gave out the most beautiful ambient moonlight," says McGarvey, "and all the lights melded with blue and green gel, so when it was switched on it didn't have the punch of a big fill light that always looks so awful on camera."

OPPOSITE A stunning piece of concept art (top) showing the submarine's propeller suspended from the forest canopy, formed the basis for the final film frame (bottom). ABOVE The "monster hunters" on the track of the MUTO in the jungle sequence. BELOW Storyboards map out the suspenseful submarine sequence.

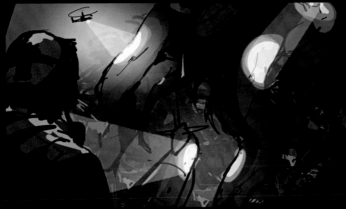

WE WATCH FROM A CIRCLING HELICOPTER AS BEAMS ILLUMINATE THE GIANT LEGS OF A MUTO

ILLUMINATING THE STRANGE SIGHT OF A GIANT PROPELLER IN THE TREES

WAR STORIES

PHILIP STRUB, THE DEPARTMENT OF DEFENSE'S entertainment liaison, recalls the Navy's reaction to the notion of them being involved in a certain monster movie: *What?! You're suggesting we work on a* Godzilla *movie?*

"I said, 'Yes I am,'" Strub recalls. "I said this was a movie with a lot of drama and character, that they were casting people who are serious actors. This wasn't like those old black-and-white movies where soldiers keep firing on the giant grasshopper, and when that doesn't work, they just keep on firing."

With the Pentagon having approved cooperation with the *Godzilla* production, Captain Russell Coons handled the logistics of "embedding" production personnel and actors on actual aircraft carriers, and other production requests, including coordinating resources, base access, and equipment with officials representing the Army, Air Force, and National Guard. Coons adds that DOD support doesn't hinge on military characters winning in all scenarios—the military service depicted simply has to exhibit the hallmarks of their training, such as courage, resilience, and adaptability. "Today the military is often portrayed fighting zombies, vampires, and aliens," Coons says with a smile, noting such recent DOD, supported productions as *Man of Steel, Iron Man*, and *Battleship*. "So it was not too extraordinary for us to assist in an engagement with a large reptile and his friends. But the public doesn't distinguish fact from fiction. If a film has our stamp of support, they need to see all of our convictions on the big screen. We want to demonstrate Navy core values to the taxpayers through the character and heroic actions of our lead EOD office on the big screen."

Separate to the DOD's involvement, the production hired James Dever as a military technical advisor. Dever was ten years old when a TV viewing of John Wayne as a fighting marine in *Sands of Iwo Jima* inspired him to become a marine. Twenty-five years later, after experi-

ences ranging from the evacuation of Saigon to Desert Storm, he retired with the rank of sergeant major and embarked on a new career as an advisor on motion picture productions. It was during his active service that he was "bitten by the movie bug" when tapped to work as a technical advisor for director Clint Eastwood's *Heartbreak Ridge*. Dever's new career as a military consultant for the movies officially started with *Green Dragon*, a 2001 drama about Vietnamese refugees who come to Camp Pendleton at the end of the Vietnam War. The makeup girl was Vietnamese, and as they talked they realized they had both been at the fall of Saigon, he as a young marine, she as a ten-year-old evacuee.

> ## "I TOLD AARON THAT HE SHOULD BE ABLE TO WALK INTO A ROOM AND IF SOMEBODY LOOKED AT HIM, THEY'D SAY, 'THAT GUY IS IN THE MILITARY.'"

For *Godzilla*, Dever ensured authenticity, from advising the art department to teaching actors playing military personnel how to embody the values of service. Dever brought his personal experience and the challenges he faced in service, such as the time in Desert Storm when they had to take a town and organize a POW camp for 4,000 prisoners. "I looked at my seniors, remembered how they taught me," he recalls of high-pressure situations. "I had great instructors, squad leaders, company commanders, and I took my experience and knowledge from them to develop myself to be a sergeant major in the Marine Corps."

Dever had to show Aaron Taylor-Johnson how to be a Navy Lieutenant EOD and advise him on specific scenes, such as when Ford Brody

jumps out of a C-17 military aircraft into the heart of San Francisco (a movie magic shot, with the actor flown on wires). "I told Aaron that he should be able to walk into a room and if somebody looked at him, they'd say, 'That guy is in the military,'" says Dever. "It's your bearing, the way you present yourself. Aaron had a thousand questions all the time—'Am I holding the weapon right, am I doing this or that right?' You know, I have never had a problem with actors. They're like sponges. They want to learn everything! As a professional soldier you train for a stressful situation, and I went over that with Aaron. You have to control and limit a lot of emotions when you are in a combat situation. Aaron did an outstanding job. The Navy should be proud their lieutenant looked so good!"

OPPOSITE BOTTOM LEFT "I cast the gentleman on the right (Wayne Geiger) just because he looked like my granddad, Ronald Herbert, who was in World War II and was in charge of the guns on a ship," says Edwards. "So it was kind of a tribute to him. I was hoping to get him in the film, but I'm not sure he made the cut. But I know my mum would have gotten a kick out of that." OPPOSITE BOTTOM RIGHT Military technical advisor James Dever marshals the troops for their next assignment. TOP A crew films the climactic HALO (High Altitude Low Opening) jump sequence on a soundstage. LEFT Taylor-Johnson suited up in preparation for the HALO jump into embattled San Francisco. ABOVE Concept art shows the military escorting a nuclear weapon through the mountains of Nevada.

cers and enlisted and close to eighty aircraft that could wreak destruction [on a target]. It's a floating city, basically."

The art department took a research trip to an aircraft carrier in San Diego, where art director Van Der Slagt shot reference photos and took measurements for exterior and interior sets. "When it came time to build the set, I knew exactly how many screens were in there and I had good images of what the nozzles and switches looked like," he says. "The interior aircraft carrier sets were created from scratch in Vancouver. There was a medical bay, a place called Serizawa's Quarters, built in the same stage space, and a room called the War Room. We built a portion of the flight deck of the aircraft carrier on the backlot so we could have a helicopter land [on it] and show some activity there. We also shot twice on aircraft carriers, and we got some terrific footage that is part of the movie."

Erik Aadahl took a sound crew to NAS North Island in San Diego, where they boarded a COD [Carrier Onboard Delivery] prop plane and were flown off the coast of Southern California, where they landed on the deck of the USS *Ronald Reagan*. For four days they recorded the sounds of the hulls, ventilation ducts, aircraft catapults, the F-18s taking off and landing from the deck.

> ## " JUST STANDING ON THAT AIRCRAFT CARRIER DECK, YOU HAVE REAL RESPECT FOR THE GUYS WHO WORK THERE EVERY DAY. "

"You hear the rumble and bow wash of a real aircraft carrier," Aadahl says, "you hear the control tower over the PA's announcing 'Clear the deck.' You hear the alarms—'Crews to stations, all hands on deck.' I'll augment it if I have to, but those straight, realistic recordings had such power. Just standing on that aircraft carrier deck, you have real respect for the men and women who work there every day, because it's the most dangerous job I can possibly imagine. When the aircraft take off, you feel it in your bones, it rumbles through your whole body. We had multiple levels of ear protection, and it still felt like you're not wearing any protection at all. There's a lot of power, a lot of noise, and a lot of danger. Fortunately, we had escorts that kept us out of the danger range, because you step in the wrong place and you'll get your legs sheared off by these big cables whiplashing across the deck that catch a jet when it's landing."

OPPOSITE TOP Concept art depicting the trainload of nuclear missiles arriving in small-town America. OPPOSITE BOTTOM Concept art of troops approaching the containment chamber of the Yucca Mountain Facility. ABOVE Sound designer Erik Aadahl picks up the roar of an aircraft carrier landing.

In the trestle bridge sequence, where Ford advances with a group of soldiers, Dever taught the actors how to move in formation and make sure their weapons and equipment were accurate. "They carried M4s with a Tech-15, a device located on the rail system that has an infrared for laser and flashlight," he says. "I worked with the guys on the way they moved and carried their weapons, the way they gave hand and arm signals to each other when they're moving forward because they don't know what's ahead of them. I had them in a staggered formation and I told them what their sectors of fire would be and who would do what if something happened. I told them to watch their weapons, to make sure you don't cross [your muzzle] behind the guy's back.

"In the movie, Aaron has a small realm, but a delicate one—he'll have to try to defuse a nuclear weapon [and do it in the vicinity of] the monster. The EOD's mission with the special forces is to move in close and get the job done. David [Strathairn] has the big realm of the operations. As the admiral, he has the overview of the whole operation."

Like Taylor-Johnson, Strathairn wanted to learn all he could to bring authenticity to the role of Admiral Stenz. "The admiral character had to inculcate a lifetime of service and also the qualities of leadership," Dever adds. "Remember, an admiral came into the service as an enlisted man and then became an officer. He's gone through all of that learning and experience. He has to show leadership in any crisis, to show he has the ability to get the job done in an outstanding manner. A leader can't be unsure."

The U.S. Navy access to aircraft carriers included research trips by production heads and opportunity to film normal activities as well as a dramatic scene of a burial at sea. "If you walked onto an aircraft carrier, you would see the might of the United States Navy," Dever notes. "You're talking about over 5,500 offi-

While on the aircraft carrier, Aadahl also picked up sounds for the nuclear facility: "There's a nuclear reactor on the carrier and there's huge vents that run all across the ship that constantly keep cooling this thing and pumping water and cycling it. The sound was massive, these really rich, deep pulsing sounds. A lot of that we were able to use for the nuclear facility."

The production also shot on the USS *Missouri* in Pearl Harbor for the sequence that opens the movie. Set in 1954, it sees military observers watching from the carrier deck as an atomic bomb is detonated at Bikini Atoll in an effort to kill Godzilla. The scene was a disturbing reminder of the atomic test at Bikini Atoll that irradiated a Japanese fishing boat and was one of the inspirations for *Gojira*.

Elizabeth Wilcox recalls the opener was shot at the end of principal photography, and they were exhausted when they arrived at the sunny beachfront set in Hawaii: "The island set was supposed to look like an idyllic life, with no awareness of the outside world. We built thatch huts and four outrigger canoes. Mostly you saw the water and beach and people drying fishnets, fishing, and weaving baskets. And then the military comes. You see the place abandoned because the military have taken the people off and they're going to release the bomb."

To Erik Aadahl, the "shape of the scene" in terms of sound was the contrast between the beauty of nature and its wrathful aspect. "One of the things I find most haunting about documentary footage from those islands, when they were testing the bombs, is they're silent," he says. "Even when they recorded sync sound, they were twelve to fifteen miles away, so the sound took a long time to get to the microphone. So when you see the explosion it's silent—it's not until the shock wave hits that you hear it. There's something so eerie about that."

THE END OF THE LINE 最終章

ONE OF THE MISCONCEPTIONS ABOUT MOVIEMAKING is that film editing is a purely post-production activity. *Godzilla* editor Bob Ducsay came on the show weeks before principal photography for meetings with the director and reviews of the previz. Everything would ultimately come through the editorial department, even the background plates shot by visual effects crews. "We're the end of the line here," Ducsay notes. "All the greatness and all the bad stuff funnels through us, and, hopefully, we enhance the stuff that's great and correct the stuff that isn't."

It was during his viewing of the director's cut that Legendary leader Jon Jashni had an epiphany: "Watching things being shot on set or watching dailies doesn't really compare to watching considered, cut sequences that absolutely verify that your filmmaker has achieved a certain tone, scale, and quality. I remember sitting in the editing room and watching Gareth show us a sampler of four or five sequences and realizing he had 'done it,' that he had somehow made this movie his own. I remember feeling excited for him and that he was well on the way to achieving what we had all been aiming for."

The amount of footage amassed for *Godzilla* was as monumental as the title character. As a yardstick, Ducsay explains that movies shot on film are traditionally measured in feet—a big movie might have 500,000 feet. *Godzilla* was shot digitally, but had the equivalent of 1.3 million feet of film—280 hours of footage, by Ducsay's estimates. "A huge part of the editor's job is to make sure no stone is left unturned, that you don't miss any gems, and the only way to do that is to watch everything," says Ducsay. "So even if you're working twelve-hour days, watching 280 hours of film becomes a multiweek endeavor. But while it's a huge bit of overhead, and really quite difficult to deal with, it gives you a lot of choices and the ability to hone a more perfect movie. You can modulate performances and modify plot points with more latitude than if you didn't have as many possibilities."

Ducsay noted that *Godzilla* was "classically made," somewhat counter to the rapid-fire cutting of most blockbusters: "I think the movie tells you how it should be cut, based on how it is photographed and the coverage. No matter how a movie is made, you can always pace scenes or slow them down. But, in the end, the movie just talks to you. Gareth has a strong vision and knows what he wants the movie to be. He wants a monster movie with a human story we truly care about, not just big explosions and monsters running around. I think making people feel something is what separates great movies from movies that are just okay, or disposable. I think everyone tries to do this. It's just hard to pull off."

Ducsay had to wear many "hats" as a film editor—story, character, the "good shot" hat. In his process, there was a general hierarchy of concerns. "I start with character; I think it's the single most important thing in a movie," he says. "Do you have compelling characters, do you like them, are they emotionally consistent? Second, there's story. I think you can have a pretty good movie with great characters and a not-so-great story, but it's pretty hard to have a movie with a great story but bad characters. And way down on the list is continuity, which is what a lot of people think is what film editors do, cutting things from one shot to the next. You can't blow off continuity, but in the list of things that matter, that's at the bottom.

"I START WITH CHARACTER; I THINK IT'S THE SINGLE MOST IMPORTANT THING IN A MOVIE."

"In an ideal world, you have a screenplay that's so airtight, and a production so pitch-perfect, you don't need to get into the gymnastics of moving things around, cutting storylines, and making radical changes. But that's never the case. For example, there were two scenes where we're on the aircraft carrier, and there was a bit of exposition in one scene that was reinforced in a later scene about Godzilla's motivation, why he had appeared and was doing what he was doing. Something the screenplay hoped was reinforcement came off as duplication, and repetition in movies is rarely a good thing. So we took the photography for those two scenes and put them into one. So even though the screenplay and production intended two scenes, by combining them you've made the movie more clear and focused."

As a visual effects movie, *Godzilla* differed greatly from a straight drama where the footage shot usually comprises the whole of the movie. In a film of this scale, so many of the shots require added CG animation and elements that are not created until months after filming wraps. Ducsay estimated that out of around 2,500 total shots covering the entire movie, more than a thousand were visual effects shots.

"One of the things about visual effects movies is [that as an editor] you have a much bigger impact on the final product, because [in post-production] you're still shooting, essentially," he says. "From a shooting standpoint, you have the ability to still effect change on maybe half the film, because the effects are still evolving. Doing visual effects is an iterative process."

Because effects shots required that live-action filming be composited with virtual material created *months* after principal photography, the visual effects work represented a discovery process for not only the effects companies but also the director and film editor. "You have material coming in where you get feedback and which interacts in a huge way with the cut, from a story and character standpoint, and also from a technical standpoint in how it fits with the live-action photography," Ducsay explains. "You have essential characters, like Godzilla, that are in the process of being created. It's as if we didn't film one of the actors, but are doing it [in post], one frame at a time."

"It's very chicken and egg," Edwards reflects during post-production on the editing of VFX shots. "We blatantly lose shots that people are working on, but you can't cut out a scene until you see what's going to be there. Then we refine the cut, get feedback, and make changes. If they [visual effects] waited until we finished that process, it would be too much of a crunch to get the film ready for the release. They have to start working on stuff now, with the expectation that a certain percentage of shots will not make the movie. But there's no way of predicting that until the stuff has already been worked out. So it's not the most efficient process, necessarily."

OPPOSITE Film editor Bob Ducsay monitors the visual effects elements. "Bob's fantastic," says Edwards. "You need an editor that's just going to be able to police the whole movie and interact with all the different departments to keep everyone on top of what's happening. Bob's a real pro at that, as well as being a great editor." RIGHT At the end of the film, Ford Brody comes face-to-face with a

GODZILLA ENCOUNTER AT COMIC-CON

AS POST-PRODUCTION BEGAN, the work of other departments ended. Art director Grant Van Der Slagt says *Godzilla* was the most challenging movie he ever worked on: "On some days, we had three, sometimes four, crews working. One day we had a film crew in Las Vegas, another shooting on an aircraft carrier, we had main unit in Vancouver, and we had a second unit running. I was extremely fortunate to have a talented crew and a very good relationship with Owen. I enjoyed the producers, the director of photography, the visual effects supervisor, and visual effects producer. I've never gotten to the end of a film and felt sad about leaving. In this case it was a wonderful experience because of the people involved. We all knew what we needed to do, and that was to make a great movie for Gareth and the studio."

It was a poignant departure for Matt Allsopp, whose growing renown had won him a coveted assignment as concept artist on J. J. Abrams' *Star Wars* production. "It felt really strange to be out of the loop," Allsopp says. "I miss it, because I got really attached to the project and got to work very closely with Gareth."

Some of the filmmakers noted the curious phenomenon of their nomadic professional lives—it all starts blending together. "Shooting amnesia" is what Mitch Dubin, from his perspective behind the camera, calls it. "You're so incredibly concentrated on that one shot you're doing and as soon as they say, 'Check the gate' and the shot is done, it just disappears. It's gone. Many times I've gone to dailies and I have no idea what I'm looking at. At the end of a movie, you always think about how many thousands of shots you did and the amount of effort it took. You go, 'I can't believe I did all this!' You just do one shot at a time. It's like a huge tapestry, and every shot is a thread."

There are lessons that stick, Dubin adds: "You really do learn something new with every movie. What's great about this industry, and my job, is every show is different. Making a shot is an evolving, organic process. One lesson from *Godzilla* is that you can take the traditional monster movie and make it new and exciting. The other lesson is that even on a movie that is so

LEFT This San Diego building was home to the Godzilla Encounter during Comic-Con 2013. **OPPOSITE PAGE** The Godzilla Encounter was an immersive experience that paid homage to the Toho tradition while looking forward to the Legendary/ Warner Bros. release.

CG dependent, so heavily prevized and storyboarded, you can still be spontaneous, as opposed to being tied down to what the visual effects are. And that came because Gareth knows visual effects so well. It renewed my confidence in the ability to improvise and have fun coming up with cool shots."

For Gareth Edwards, the transition from production to post was jolting. After the last shot in Hawaii, he was rushed to the airport for a flight to San Diego and Comic-Con 2013, where he was whisked to Hall H and the *Godzilla* panel he shared with Aaron Taylor-Johnson, Bryan Cranston, and Elizabeth Olsen. "You've literally wrapped, finished the last shot from an eighty-five-day shoot on a massive Hollywood film, and you fly straight to San Diego and a room of 6,000 people," he says. "It was really nerve-racking. I was just praying we could get through Hall H and me not make an idiot of myself."

Comic-Con 2013 was an opportunity to unveil another compelling bit of footage, this time an actual scene from the movie—the nighttime face-off between Godzilla and the MUTO in Hawaii. One of the earliest of the key scenes developed in the screenplay, storyboards, and previz, the dramatic shot was brought to life by

DNeg and featured a view outside the wall-size airport windows as the creatures roar and chaos erupts.

In addition to the panel at Comic-Con, Legendary also produced the Godzilla Encounter, a fan-friendly promotion at a downtown venue that served up Godzilla memorabilia and offered a unique thrill ride experience. Visitors were whisked through a nuclear control room in crisis before taking an imperiled elevator to an overlook where they witnessed a rampaging Godzilla.

Jon Jashni characterizes the Godzilla Encounter as a special gift to the annual party that is Comic-Con. "Comic-Con feels a bit like a family reunion every year," Jashni says, "and we just wanted to bring something really great to the potluck. At Legendary, we feel we're in the business of creating experiences, whether we transport audiences through film or, in the case of the Godzilla Encounter, a live venue. This experience had to fit the same high standards we set for the movie, and we felt it would be much easier to immerse our fans in the experience by having it reside offsite. We leased a warehouse [in downtown San Diego] that was slated for demolition, and our team was able to secretly build it from the inside out. The experience that was

OPPOSITE The male MUTO rises in another frame from the Comic-Con sneak peek. This shot was ultimately cut from the final movie. BELOW Godzilla battles the winged MUTO at the Honolulu airport in this final film frame glimpsed by audiences at Comic-Con. "This was shot the first day that we started filming," says Edwards. "We had hundreds of people in this giant convention center in Vancouver. It took hours, and I felt really guilty that so much money was being spent on just one shot in the movie, but I think it's one of the most memorable moments in the whole film."

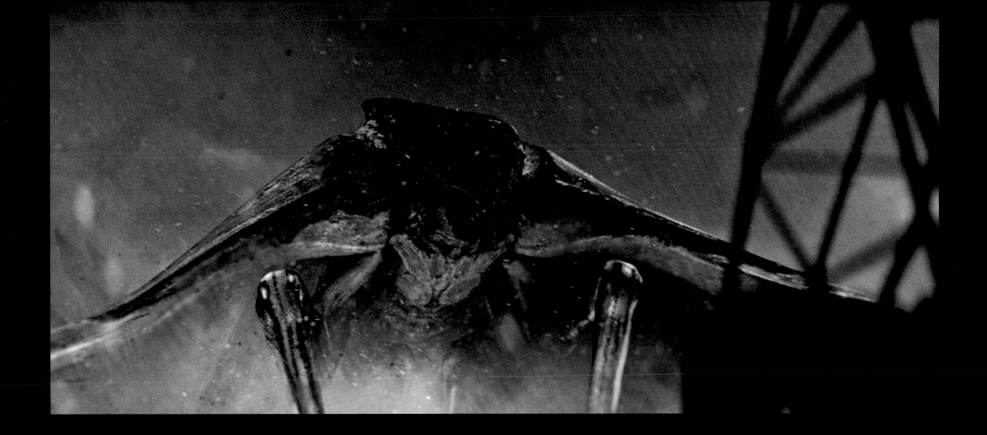

created allowed fans to taste, feel, and stand in a tangible world that was rooted in canon but also went to an entirely new place."

The mastermind behind planning and executing the Godzilla Encounter was Emily Castel, whose marketing agency, FIVE33, was a leader in producing special events for major film releases. "We loved what she did for us on *Pacific Rim* and *Godzilla* and we admired what she was doing with different franchises for other studios around town. The truth is that we got a bit jealous," Jashni says with a smile. "We didn't want to share Emily and her team—so we bought her company, and Emily is now the chief marketing officer for Legendary."

As part of his Comic-Con visit, Gareth Edwards was taken to the Godzilla Encounter, along with Taylor-Johnson, Cranston, and Olsen: "It was strange because some of the sets they had were from the MUTO facility, the crow's nest part of the film. I'd gotten away from the film in terms of the filming and all that craziness. It was my first day off in six months. It was like taking an alcoholic on a tour of a brewery, the worst possible thing. But it was also incredibly inspiring—I

actually wish I had gone through the Godzilla Encounter *before* I started filming. I left, thinking, 'Godzilla has a pretty amazing legacy. I'd love to make a Godzilla movie one day. That would be fantastic!' And suddenly you nudge yourself, 'Oh, yeah. I have!'"

"AT LEGENDARY, WE FEEL WE'RE IN THE BUSINESS OF CREATING EXPERIENCES, WHETHER WE TRANSPORT AUDIENCES THROUGH FILM OR, IN THE CASE OF THE GODZILLA ENCOUNTER, A LIVE VENUE."

PART THREE

CREATION

MONSTER BLOODBATH

"Well, you couldn't really have a Godzilla movie without the great destruction scenes. It's so great. It's gonna be a bloodbath. Monster bloodbath." —BRYAN CRANSTON

THE LATE RAY HARRYHAUSEN often recalled watching the original release of *King Kong* as a boy and how that viewing at showman Sid Grauman's famed Chinese Theatre on Hollywood Boulevard changed his life: "It was just overwhelming. Half the charm of it was I didn't know how it was done. It was obvious it wasn't a man in a gorilla suit, but I didn't know a thing about stop-motion. But it wasn't just the technical expertise, it was the structure of the story. For the first half hour, it took you by the hand from the mundane world and into the most outrageous fantasy that's ever been put on the screen."[7]

IT'S INSANE. I WOULDN'T SAY WE HAVE IT EASY NOW, BUT HAVING HAD MY STINT IN VISUAL EFFECTS, PEOPLE DO UNDERESTIMATE HOW HARD IT IS TO DO THIS STUFF."

Harryhausen learned the secrets of stop-motion animation—the meticulous manipulation and filming of articulated puppets a frame at a time—and went on to produce some outrageous fantasies of his own. "There's a level of genius to what he did," marvels Gareth Edwards, who grew up loving Harryhausen classics from the seminal *The Beast from 20,000 Fathoms* to *Clash of the Titans*. "It doesn't add up how you can animate every snake on Medusa's head, individually, a frame at a time on your own. I can't comprehend it. It's insane. I wouldn't say we have it easy now, but having had my stint in visual effects, people do underestimate how hard it is to do this stuff."

Edwards recalled being on a BBC crew that went to interview Harryhausen at his home in London, some eight years ago. During a break, while the crew was busy, Edwards was asked to keep Harryhausen busy. Edwards asked Harryhausen if he had seen the Internet trailer for Peter Jackson's *King Kong* remake, featuring a CG Kong. When Harryhausen said he hadn't seen it, Edwards realized he had his laptop in his bag. "I pulled out my laptop and headphones and played Ray Harryhausen this trailer," he recalls. "Nobody else understood the significance of it. I felt really honored that I was getting to be the person to do it. I half expected him to have an issue with it, but he was blown away. He seemed really excited. Toho's *Godzilla* owes a lot to *The Beast from 20,000 Fathoms*. I believe it was the success of that and the rerelease of *King Kong* that got Toho excited about trying to do something similar. So Ray Harryhausen, in some way, helped kick-start our version of *Godzilla* as well."

RIGHT This concept art captures the peril as the HALO team parachutes into the midst of the Godzilla and MUTO battle. "There's a fine line between doing things that are exciting and just stupid when you're doing a film like this," says Edwards. "You don't want a scenario to be so insane that it just feels like you're making a cheesy popcorn movie. So we were trying to do a gritty, realistic version of what a HALO jump would be like."

Although both stop-motion and CG creature models are articulated with spinal and skeletal systems that are key to their respective animation, the virtual version has a freedom of movement Harryhausen envied. "The spinal and skeletal system is key to defining the articulation points that define how things are going to move," MPC supervisor Rocheron explains. "For Godzilla's shoulders, where do you position the bone? Where does his shoulder rotate? The way you design the skeleton is the way it's going to move. Once we have the skeleton in place, we start attaching muscle. You have completely different behavior on Godzilla's thigh, for example. It's a much more defined muscle structure than on his legs and back where his scales are thicker. Once we have our layers of skeleton and muscle, the second phase is adding layers of fat and things to make the skin move and deform as realistically as possible. That's where our animation team starts, because we have to do a lot of motion studies for Godzilla and the other creatures as well. Motion studies are an important component when you create creatures, because they define their attitude."

Rocheron notes the life of an effects shot across ten-seconds of film can require two to three months of work. The key is being clear at every stage of the process. Stage one is getting the director to sign off on preliminary animation—are the framing and blocking okay, is he happy with the way Godzilla moves? The next iteration might then add details of movement, "all the refinement of the acting, really," Rocheron says. "Then we start to actually light him and integrate him in shots. Working with a director like Gareth, who actually did visual effects and understands the process, is tremendously helpful. It makes it smoother in achieving all the mini-goals we have on every shot."

> ## "MOTION STUDIES ARE AN IMPORTANT COMPONENT WHEN YOU CREATE CREATURES, BECAUSE THEY DEFINE THEIR ATTITUDE."

MPC's creature work included the MUTO models it handed off to Double Negative for the trestle bridge sequence and other shots. "We did the animation, lighting, and rendering in the trestle bridge shots; MPC did the creature build and the texturing," says DNeg's Ken McGaugh. "All of that is fairly transportable between companies, but the 'LookDev' and rigging, which defines how the creature deforms when it moves, tends to rely on proprietary

LEFT Godzilla on the offensive in the San Francisco Marina District. Battered landmarks include the historic Palace of Fine Arts (foreground) and the Financial District's Transamerica Pyramid (far right).

techniques that every company does differently. In those cases, we do have to create a new rig, but MPC gave us turntable images and moving footage tests, and we replicated that so it was consistent between their sequences and our sequences."

"GARETH SAID, 'I DON'T WANT TO REHEARSE, LET'S SHOOT IT DOCUMENTARY STYLE.'"

For the third act battle in San Francisco, MPC dramatically expanded upon the sets on the old *Watchmen* backlot by building a virtual city. MPC utilized its cutting-edge version of what is called "pan and tile." The effect traditionally utilized a "motion control" camera, designed for programmable and repeatable moves, to film a specific portion, or "tile," of a location. Taking the mosaic of tiles into the computer allowed effects artists to seamlessly connect them and allow for movement in the virtual environment—the "pan" part of the equation. For its version, MPC had their automated, high-resolution EnviroCam—originally developed for the Smallville battle in *Man of Steel*—that allowed them to capture a 360-degree still camera spherical panorama of a location.

Five EnviroCam teams, on two separate trips, shot thousands of still references, with angles often favoring rooftop views. The teams followed the battle plan mapped out in The Third Floor's previz, taking in the sweep of the monster fight from Chinatown to the Financial District and on to the bayfront Embarcadero and Fisherman's Wharf.

To make for a seamless blend of live-action and virtual, MPC followed the director of photography's lead in his lighting of the foreground plate. The battle itself would play out at night with flashes of lightning and thunder, with McGarvey flashing frames of light that would be replicated with what Rocheron calls virtual "artistic lighting." "We put a little bit of fire behind Godzilla, because it's going to silhouette his back, and tweaked the position of the moonlight so it added a little bit of rim light onto his fins," he says. "What Seamus was doing on set with the actors, we did on the creatures and the virtual environment. We definitely took creative license, but always tried to be consistent with the foreground. Something that's also handy on a set for a project like *Godzilla*, that has so many visual effects, is using previz as a guide. Seamus could look at it and go, 'Okay, Godzilla is going to be in front of the characters and they're going to be in his shadow.' So he'd light them in shadow. That's where, on set, you have collaboration on a shot-by-shot basis."

To create the virtual destruction, MPC used its in-house software, appropriately called Kali—the Hindu goddess whose attributes include change and destruction. "Our Kali software approaches destruction in a very world-based way," says Rocheron. "So we say, 'This is made of concrete and this is the way concrete behaves.' And with the concrete we add supporting structures that affect how the concrete breaks. A lot of what we were doing is art directing the destruction. We basically approached it the way [a physical special effects department] would do. When they destroy a miniature, they put charges inside at a couple points and define the weaker point because you want the building to collapse and fall screen right, for example. But we do that all in the computer."

RIGHT HALO troopers fall back to the crest of Nob Hill, concept art. **BELOW** Storyboards outline a sequence where the troopers witness a major dustup between Godzilla and the male MUTO. **FOLLOWING PAGES** Godzilla is loose in North Beach! "There's something great about San Francisco in that the streets rise to a hill," says Edwards. "I like the idea of the creature on the hill; it feels kind of like a medieval thing of, like, taking the castle on the hill, like that's the mission of the soldiers."

WE SEE DOWN THE HILL AS THEY CONTINUE TO RUN WHEN...

SHOT CONTINUED. GODZILLA'S FOOT SLAMS INTO THE STREET AHEAD

WE TILT UP FROM THE

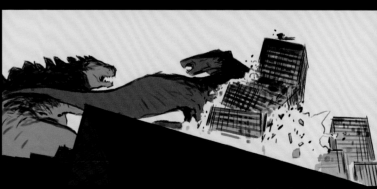

ALO TEAM TOWARDS...

SHOT CONTINUED. GODZILLA FIGHTING THE MALE

THE BUILDING COLLAPSES ON GODZILLA

medical triage staged in a Vancouver stadium, with the set decorating department putting up the tents and providing emergency medical supplies. One set decoration person spent several weeks creating poignant "missing person" notes, the phone numbers and pleas scribbled on the backs of receipts or pieces of cardboard, the posted photos of missing loved ones.

"Some of the shots in this movie were very structured and pre-planned," Mitch Dubin notes. "We had storyboards and previz and Gareth had very specific ideas of how to film it. For other stuff, like the final reunion, Gareth said, 'I don't want to rehearse, let's shoot it documentary style.' We were working with a lot of extras and he didn't want to do it over and over and lose the emotional reality of what they were doing, because they're also reuniting with their families. It was filmed handheld. It was pretty moving, having these extras do their thing."

As shots progressed in post, visual effects supervisor Jim Rygiel sent composite shots to McGarvey so he could make sure the photographic tone stayed consistent. "It was important to preserve the in-camera naturalism," McGarvey notes. "That was absolutely key to making this film feel like you're there and that it's not just a visual effects movie. There's a kind of danger to go into that vivid visual effects thing where people are proud of how great it looks, but we wanted to feel this is happening for real."

> ## I LOVED THE IDEA OF THE ROOSTER CALLING THE ADVENT OF THE DAWN—SOMETHING ABOUT THAT REMINDED ME OF GODZILLA, THAT HE'S CALLING THE DAWN OF A NEW ERA.

Another important factor in creating a vividly realistic atmosphere was the work of the sound design department. Having begun with his "central element" of dried ice on metal, Erik Aadahl continued to explore a full range of Godzilla roars to meet the complexity of scenes like the battle in San Francisco. "The metals I used [initially] were kind of sheet metal," he says. "But for a long time I wanted to use more of an instrument shaped metal, like ventilation ducting, to get that vocal cord–type anatomy. So the roar wound up being this big tube that was maybe two and a half feet in diameter and six feet long, bellowing and shrieking and resonating. That gave me a nice medium range."

To Aadahl, the art of sound design was to keep it "singular"—too many layers were akin to mixing too many colors in a paint palette and ending up with brown. "In the same way, too many frequencies get really muddy," he says. "I tried to find things I could work against those metal sounds that sounded cohesive, part of the whole."

The low end of Godzilla's rumbling inflection was a microphone he placed inside the terra cotta pot of a backyard plant and then scraped over concrete, creating a grinding, rumbling sound he then imported into a computer: "I compressed

it a little bit, took out some of the high end but enhanced the low end, and blended those together so you got both the shriek, but also the earthquake-like rumbling power, the force of nature, that element that rumbles your gut."

A subtler Godzilla sound came serendipitously when Aadahl was working at a studio and heard what sounded like the groan of a big creature: "I instantly grabbed my recording rig and ran all around the building and found it—this big wooden palette with a thousand pounds of computer equipment piled on it and movers were pushing it over a polished concrete floor. And it was creating this big, deep groaning, stuttering sound. That became one of the most emotive creature sounds for Godzilla."

It's always an exploration, Aadahl emphasizes. On a honeymoon trip to Kauai, he brought along his recording rig because *Godzilla* had a Hawaii section. He was intrigued by the ubiquitous chickens and roosters and began playing with rooster noises as another potential tonal range. "I loved the idea of the rooster calling the advent of the dawn—something about that reminded me of Godzilla, that he's calling the dawn of a new era," he says. "I started with slowing it down so it doesn't sound like a rooster, but there are so many little frequencies or details. You come up with an idea and play with it for a while, and maybe it sticks or doesn't. But that's the process—experiment, play, and evolve."

The sound designer wanted the same scale of power he was applying to Godzilla to inform the MUTOs, but he wanted them "sonically different." He played less with "shrieks" and more with a "guttural bellow" approach. "I used a very territorial bird that gave me some awesome and powerful vocals," he says. "I slowed that down and found that sweet spot with the speed where it sounded gigantic. I also used elephant trunk blows, this big air sound with a big stutter to it, like you could hear the rush of air resonating within the trunk. I slowed them down, and those are a lot of the MUTO's breathing sounds."

There was an underlying biological component based on bioacoustics, a field that explores the notion that animal sounds are not meaningless noises. "We're only now starting to understand there's this whole rich world of music and language and communication in the animal kingdom," he says. "It's kind of a story point in the film, that there's an intelligence there."

INTO THE DIGITAL REALM デジタル界へ

WARNER BROS. STUDIO IN BURBANK still retains a sprawling backlot. A walk across the lot takes a visitor to Warner Village, a small-town neighborhood backlot of two-story homes that doubles as office space. Number 183 was home to *Godzilla* post-production. The first floor was where Jim Rygiel's visual effects department set up shop, the second floor was home to editorial, and the building's garage was the "mad scientist" place, as Bob Ducsay put it, where The Third Floor and Pixel Pirates, another effects company brought onto the project, were steeped in the postviz conceptual phase.

"A friend of mine explained the difference between production and post-production is that when you're filming, you start with the real world and reduce and refine it down to the specific shot and bits of information in the frame," Gareth Edwards explains. "In the digital realm you start with nothing; you have to build and add everything into the shot. The upside to the computer is you can do anything. The downside is you have to do everything. So, you have to add the grease on the bolt on the [CG] helicopter in the background." On an unusually cool and overcast late September day in 2013, the *Godzilla* post team was planning on how to do just that.

Jim Rygiel and visual effects producer Allen Maris are in a dark room for the daily visual effects shot review, looking at monitors with three coordinators, their laptops out as they type in the various notes. The shots are predominately from Double Negative. At this stage all the shots are still rough, with postviz teams slamming out rough CG comps to go with the live action.

It is a wide range of shots. The opening Bikini Atoll sequence with actors playing villagers on the beachfront set in Hawaii is comped with CG waves being displaced as a rough computer-generated submarine surfaces. The MUTO rises from the nuclear power plant pit as Bryan Cranston's Joe Brody watches from a catwalk. Trestle bridge shots include train tracks through a tunnel and a distant explosion, with a menacing, greyscale-shaded MUTO at the bridge. A CG Chinook helicopter is hovering above Aaron Taylor-Johnson's Ford Brody as he picks his way through rubble. A Las Vegas firefighter is gazing past a broken wall to the matte-painted wreckage of Caesar's Palace. Low-resolution CG images of Godzilla's spiny fins are breaking the choppy water before the creature dives under an aircraft carrier. . . .

The talk turns to Godzilla himself. "Godzilla is probably darker than in the past, the essence of charcoal and carbon," says Rygiel. "He's a lot more craggy." There's a bit of green in there, but it's a dark green, it's more ominous. He's staying a little bit more with reality, where there's an electrical spark. In fact, we saw a shot yesterday where he had a big glow around his head and we

sort of took that out, so it's just more like a taser blast. MPC is doing Godzilla, and he's looking *unbelievable*!"

The male MUTO breaking the restraints at the nuclear facility gets some Bob Ducsay commentary—it is moving in too much of an east-west direction. Edwards stands up from a couch and moves like he is trying to break invisible bonds—the MUTO needs to appear as if it is *straining* to escape, and should not look locked in.

Another Q-Zone shot shows Cranston in the shadow of the MUTO's destruction, with low-res CG cranes starting to collapse. "Some things are moving too fast," Rygiel notes.

The director's session runs through the roster of shots and concludes in high spirits. "This is very encouraging, this stuff," Ducsay exults. "It's very exciting."

"IN THE DIGITAL REALM YOU START WITH NOTHING; YOU HAVE TO BUILD AND ADD EVERYTHING INTO THE SHOT."

Back upstairs in his spacious editing room, Ducsay pulls up the seminal Comic-Con teaser on his monitors. The camera slowly pans across the crushed and collapsed buildings, and over it all is the heavy voice of the father of the atomic bomb recalling Vishnu, incarnation of death and destroyer of worlds—no text on screen to identify the voice, just the feeling of a newscaster broadcasting from the aftermath of Armageddon. As Godzilla turns in the smoke and roars, Ducsay gestures to the director, who is standing in the doorway—*this* is how the matte painting of the ruins of Caesar's Palace should look.

OPPOSITE The mighty Godzilla, final film frame. RIGHT Concept art of a MUTO tearing up Chinatown. "At one point, the MUTO burrowed its way out of the ground in San Francisco, but it's hard to believe that something could burrow its way across America in just a day or so," says Edwards. "So even though it's a cool image, it just felt unbelievable." FOLLOWING PAGES The insect-like HALO team, beneath the notice of the towering combatants, try to steal away with the nuclear warhead. "I always felt this was the mice with the slice of cheese and the cats above them," says Edwards.

STOP

ALL WAY

Washington

POWELL

CABLE CAR
CORNER

FRESH DONUT

ESPRESSO
CAPPUCCINO

TROPICAL
ICE CREAM

MASON St

ACADEMIC STANDARDS
STEEPER THAN THIS HILL

SAN FRANCISCO MUNICIPAL RAILWAY

It was always about how to tell the story. Ducsay emphasizes three stages of storytelling in a movie production: There's the movie you write, the movie you film, and the final movie that comes together in post. It was about the details and the razor-thin line between what works and doesn't work, between good intentions and the reality of what you have in hand. At this point, Ducsay notes, the director has already seen his editor's cut of the entire movie. Now, they are in the middle of cutting the director's cut before it is shown to the studio.

"About two weeks after principal photography, Gareth watched the movie for the first time," Ducsay says, referring to his editor's cut. "So, the movie exists, but it's still unformed. We go back through all

"THE MUTO NEEDS TO APPEAR AS IF IT IS *STRAINING* TO ESCAPE, AND SHOULD NOT LOOK LOCKED IN."

the sequences, taking the director's notes in a collaborative process. Cutting a movie is very complex storytelling. When you begin, it's a discovery. You don't really know the characters or the tone—you're really seeing it all for the first time. You're learning what the movie is about.

"Movies are a handmade thing, a new R&D project every single time. It takes a while to figure everything out, and you learn more and more about what the movie is and how the characters are supposed to work and the best way to implement the director's vision. And it's a frame at a time, a shot at a time, a moment at a time. . . ."

LEFT As the winged MUTO is peppered with Air Force fire, San Francisco burns in the distance.

"THIS IS GOING TO WORK, THIS IS GOING TO BE COOL . . ."

THERE WERE TIMES AT NIGHT, when Gareth Edwards walked out of #183 Warner Village and down the deserted backlot, that it felt as if he had stepped into an apocalyptic movie where humankind had vanished and he was the sole survivor. Edwards had come to America to make a Hollywood movie—"I spend the whole time thinking I'm in one big movie set"—he recalled of his initial culture shock. Working in an actual backlot set was the ultimate surreal touch.

But even as he reached post-production, Edwards was still looking over his shoulder: "I still feel like someone is going to jump out and shout, 'Surprise! You're not really making a movie. It's all been a trick!' And I'd be, like, 'Of course. I knew deep down it was just pretend. Of course I'm not really making *Godzilla*. That would be crazy.'"

As Edwards moved into the visual effects, editing, and scoring of the film, he saluted his cast. "I was amazed with everybody," he says. "I'm kind of honored they all wanted to do it."

It was late September, still early in *Godzilla* post-production, and Edwards was in the middle of getting his director's cut ready. He reflected on the final phase of the production as he sat down with a plate of pizza in the back booth of a noisy cafeteria on the Warner Bros. lot: "I used to describe the making of *Monsters* as the worst time of my life. But when the film did okay and led to things like this, I look back and it was like some crazy, fun adventure. It's like your brain kind of deletes all the pain. I would definitely describe *Godzilla* as the hardest thing I've ever had to do. But I think, given time, I'll end up rose-tinting it all.

"I couldn't be more excited because we've got the composer, Alexandre Desplat. He's just a genius and has that perfect balance for this film. It's great when a composer comes in and [takes the temp music] and makes it all better and defined and from the same voice.

"Making a film, or editing, at this stage is like finding a jigsaw puzzle but you've lost the box so you can't see the picture. You're kind of looking at the pieces, figuring it out. Suddenly you go, 'Oh, that's not a corner piece, is it?' So you swap it around so it fits a lot better. Bob did an amazing job assembling the movie, the first cut I saw after we finished filming. It was very watchable and exciting, because you could see what it was going to be, sort of. And it was like, how do we get there? We have this great release date, thank God, the beginning of the summer. Everything works backwards from there. Even the trailer, we've got to lock it next week, and there's not a single effects shot started on it, you know? I would ask, 'Is this normal?' Most people go, 'This is normal. Don't worry about it; it's always crazy and really busy.'

RIGHT Concept art showing a helicopter view across to Telegraph Hill and Coit Tower. "I love the subjective view of being in a helicopter, but in the final film we couldn't have helicopters," says Edwards. "It would ruin the storyline, because the EMP has stopped anything being able to fly near the MUTOs."

imes you try something different and it doesn't work at all. Sometimes you play it safe and that doesn't work either. It's a real tricky balance. I think when you're the filmmaker, you can't see the woods for the trees when you're in the thick of it. I know what I want shots to do, but it doesn't mean we've got it that way. Reality comes along and it's full of compromise, and things don't necessarily happen the way you picture them happening.

"Pre-production is like the dream, filming is the punishment or the price you pay, and post-production is the reward. There are many different things that happen in editing, and one of the most interesting is you start removing all the bits you don't like and seeing if the film still holds together. What is sort of frustrating and, in retrospect, fully obvious is I have a tendency to get excited about a shot within a scene. I'll want to turn that shot into a sequence, and it'll grow like a cancer and expand as part of the body of the film. I'll get interested and excited about all these visual excursions. The problem is, I'm finding now, you can't have them all in the movie. As great as some of them might be, all that really matters is the experience as a whole. It's not about the individual pieces. Story is king, and if you don't keep getting back to the story of the film, it feels like a rambling old man who can't stick to the point.

"I find music one of the most inspiring things. Early in the pre-production, before I made the presentation to Warner Bros., I was staying in Santa Monica. I used to walk around at night with my headphones on and listen to soundtracks,

Odyssey, the music when they go though the Star Gate. And I used to look up into the night sky and picture tiny little people falling, and it used to give me shivers. And I thought, 'That's got to be in the movie.'

"PRE-PRODUCTION IS LIKE THE DREAM, FILMING IS THE PUNISHMENT OR THE PRICE YOU PAY, AND POST-PRODUCTION IS THE REWARD."

"There's the sequence we call the HALO jump, where Ford jumps out of this C-17 and into the third act. I was basically trying to find an angle on it that didn't make it feel like a clichéd Hollywood scene where soldiers are going to jump out of a plane and be heroes. I wanted to find a way of doing that, for better or worse, in a way that felt a bit different—that music was the hook-in for me. I drew a few crappy ideas for shots and then sat down with Matt Allsopp. Matt made them amazing and added twice as many ideas. And The Third Floor and Eric were there. And they very quickly put them in order with that music on top. And we all got chills. 'This is going to work, this is going to be cool. . . .'"

BELOW AND OPPOSITE Storyboar sequence for the fiery HALO jump. " just sat with Matt Allsopp and drew some really rough ideas for shots, an he turned them into these little work of art," says Edwards. "The Third Floo turned it into this great little animatio sequence, we whacked the music ove it, put a little prayer on it from the gu inside the plane, and, even in its crud form, it gave me goose bumps. When th studio saw it, they felt the same way, an so it's pretty much never changed from the first iteration—we just went an shot exactly what was prevized."

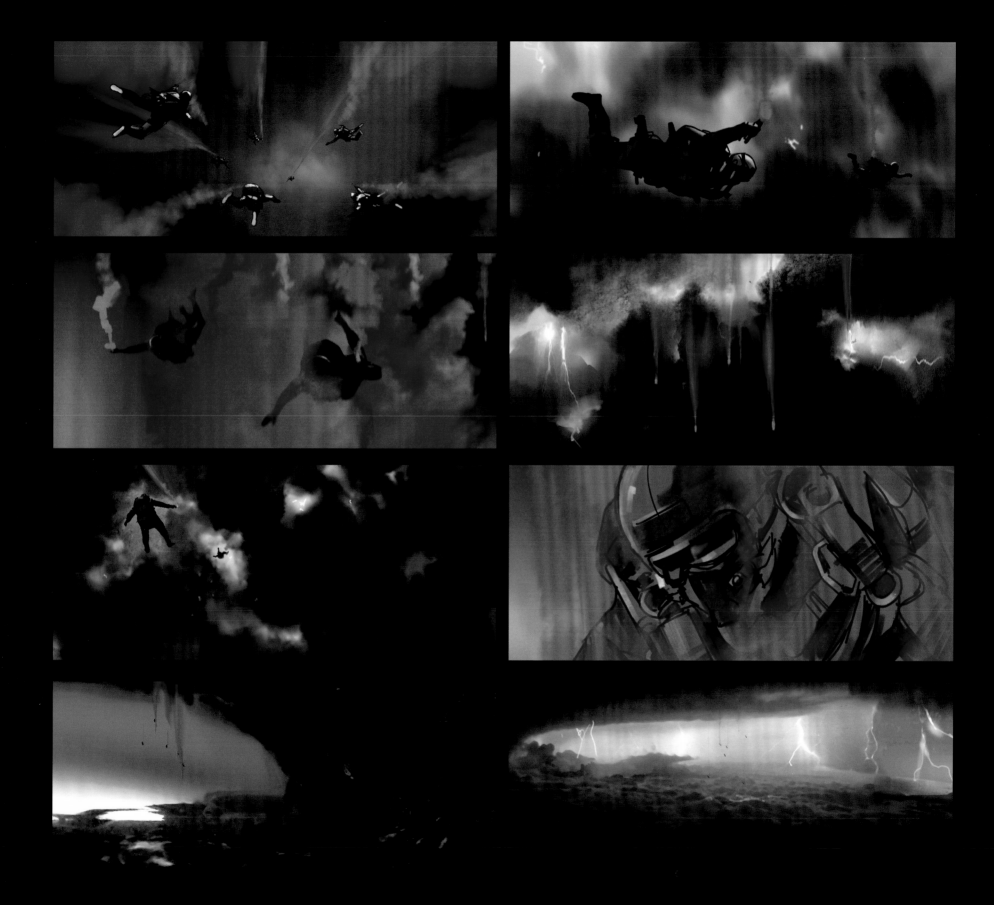

INSIGHT
EDITIONS

PO Box 3088 • San Rafael, CA 94912
www.insighteditions.com

Find us on Facebook: www.facebook.com/InsightEditions
Follow us on Twitter: @insighteditions

LEGENDARY

Published by Insight Editions, San Rafael, California, in 2014. No part of this book
may be reproduced in any form without written permission from the publisher.

Library of Congress Cataloging-in-Publication Data available.

ISBN: 978-1-60887-344-9

Publisher: Raoul Goff
Acquisitions Editor: Robbie Schmidt
Editor: Chris Prince
Art Director: Chrissy Kwasnik
Interior Layout & Design: Kristoffer Branco & Chrissy Kwasnik
Cover Design: Kristoffer Branco
Production Editor: Rachel Anderson
Production Manager: Jane Chinn
Editorial Assistant: Elaine Ou

INSIGHT EDITIONS would like to thank Gareth Edwards, Josh Anderson, Shane Thompson, Elaine Piechowski,
Shannon Triplett, Emily Castel, Mansi Patel, Jamie Kampel, Nick Gligor, Jill Benscoter, Spencer Douglas,
Peter Stone, Steve Fogelson, Stephanie Mente, and Miwako Nishizawa. MUTOs gracias!

ROOTS of PEACE   REPLANTED PAPER

Insight Editions, in association with Roots of Peace, will plant two trees for each tree used in the manufacturing of this book.
Roots of Peace is an internationally renowned humanitarian organization dedicated to eradicating land mines worldwide and
converting war-torn lands into productive farms and wildlife habitats. Roots of Peace will plant two million fruit and nut trees
in Afghanistan and provide farmers there with the skills and support necessary for sustainable land use.

Manufactured in Hong Kong by Insight Editions

10 9 8 7 6 5 4 3 2

NOTES

1. Kai Bird and Martin J. Sherwin, *American Prometheus: The Triumph and Tragedy of
   J. Robert Oppenheimer* (New York: Alfred A. Knopf, 2005), 291, 307–309.
2. Bruce Lanier Wright, *Yesterday's Tomorrows: The Golden Age of Science Fiction Posters*
   (Dallas: Taylor Publishing Company, 1993), 68.
3. Bird and Sherwin, *American Prometheus*, 309. The authors include a comment from an
   Oppenheimer friend who questioned the authenticity of this memory, suggesting it was
   one of Oppenheimer's "priestly exaggerations."
4. San Diego Comic-Con International "Events Guide," 75.
5. Peter Aperlo, *Watchmen: The Film Companion* (London: Titan Books, 2009), 29.
6. Mark Cotta Vaz, *Living Dangerously: The Adventures of Merian C. Cooper, Creator of
   King Kong* (New York: Villard Books, 2005), 211.
7. Vaz, *Living Dangerously*, 237.

ACKNOWLEDGMENTS

A Godzilla-size roar of appreciation to Gareth Edwards, who was a champion
for this book. And more of the same to the talented filmmakers who also
gave of their time and provided exclusive interviews for this book: Legendary
founder and producer Thomas Tull, Legendary president and producer Jon
Jashni, executive producer Alex Garcia, producer Brian Rogers, producer
Mary Parent, screenwriter Max Borenstein, concept artist Matt Allsopp, The
Third Floor previz lead Eric Carney, cinematographer Seamus McGarvey,
camera operator Mitch Dubin, supervising art director Grant Van Der Slagt,
set decorator Elizabeth Wilcox, costume designer Sharen Davis, military
technical advisor James Dever, Department of Defense liaison Philip Strub,
director of the Navy Office of Information West Captain Russell Coons, visual
effects supervisor Jim Rygiel, MPC visual effects supervisor Guillaume
Rocheron, Double Negative visual effects supervisor Ken McGaugh, sound
designer Erik Aadahl, and the guy at the end of the line, Bob Ducsay.

On the personal side, my special appreciation to my steadfast and true
agent, John Silbersack, and his superb assistant, Anna Qu, and to Chris
Prince at Insight Editions, who was always on top of everything and, yes, a
prince of a fellow. A Godzilla roar as well for Josh Anderson, Shane Thompson,
Spencer Douglas, and Jill Benscoter at Warner Bros., Alex Garcia's assistant
Shirit Bradley, Jon Jashni's assistant Amanda Sifuentes Villarreal, Mary
Parent's assistant Marcieanna Klaustermeyer, and those amazing people at
#183 Warner Village, including Gareth's stellar assistant, Shannon Triplett,
and to J. T. Billings (for getting me on the road to the Bob Hope Airport). And a
bow of respect to Thomas Tull and the pros who connected us: Sarah Brandt,
Paul Pflug, and Sheana Knighton. And thanks to Mike Stoltz at Comic-Con!

Love and all of it to my mother, Bettylu Vaz, who did her usual great
proofreading job—nothing gets by you! This work is also dedicated to
my father, August Mark Vaz, a schoolteacher who touched and changed
hundreds—thousands—of lives and truly lived the *It's a Wonderful Life*
scenario. See you and our ancestors on the other side of the rainbow, padre.

And to Mike Wigner, San Francisco's greatest bicycle messenger: We're
going to have to watch out for rampaging monsters when we head to North
Beach, but it'll be cool—it's a wrap, see you at Vesuvio.

—M.C.V.

CREDITS

Erik Aadahl, Matt Allsopp, Andrew Baker, Chris Beach, Aaron Beck,
Rob Bilson, Rob Bliss, Brent Boates, Gavin Bocquet, Phil Bray (on-set
photographer—Hawaii), Greg Broadmore, Ryan Church, David Clarke,
John Coven, James Crockett, Brian Cunningham, Sharen Davis,
Eddie Del Rio, Ross Dempster, John Dickenson, Summer Dietz,
Joël Dos Reis Viegas, Gareth Edwards, Patrick Faulwetter, Gina Flanagan,
Warren Flanagan, Kirsten Franson, Kimberley French (on-set photographer),
Doane Gregory (temp on-set photographer), Trevor Hensley, Dan Hermansen,
Doug Higgins, Ian Joyner, Jaclyn Kenney, Vance Kovacs, Sébastien Larroudé,
Dominic Lavery, David Levy, Andrew Li, Scott Meehan, Véronique Meignaud,
Steve Messing, Kan Mistic, Steve Munson, John Park, Owen Paterson,
Scott Patton, Christian Pearce, Vicki Pui, Erin Sinclair, Erik Tiemens,
Shannon Triplett, Grant Van Der Slagt, Simon Webber, Nathaniel West,
and Harrison Yurkiw.

Special thanks to the teams at DNeg, Legacy, MPC, Steambot,
and Weta Workshop.